Her Bestfriend

Barbara Thompson

Copyright © 2024 by Barbara Thompson

All rights reserved.

No portion of this book may be reproduced in any form without written permission from the publisher or author, except as permitted by U.S. copyright law.

Contents

1. Chapter 1 Part 1: Academy Bound   1
2. Chapter 1 Part 2: Academy Bound   4
3. Chapter 1 Part 3: Academy Bound   7
4. Chapter 1 Part 4: Academy Bound   12
5. Doki Doki Magic Love Academy: The Prince   16
6. Doki Doki Magic Love Academy: The Knight   20
7. Doki Doki Magic Love Academy: The Wizard   24
8. Doki Doki Magic Love Academy: The Professor   28
9. Doki Doki Magic Love Academy: The Aristocrat   31
10. Chapter 2 Part 1: The Game Begins   34
11. Chapter 2 Part 2: The Game Begins   38
12. Chapter 2 Part 3: The Game Begins   42
13. Chapter 2 Part 4: The Game Begins   46
14. Chapter 3 Part 1: Of Magic and Men   53
15. Chapter 3 Part 2: Of Magic and Men   58

16.	Chapter 3 Part 3: Of Magic and Men	62
17.	Chapter 3 Part 4: Of Magic and Men	67
18.	Chapter 4 Part 1: Grinding Stats	72
19.	Chapter 4 Part 2: Grinding Stats	76
20.	Chapter 4 Part 3: Grinding Stats	81
21.	Chapter 4 Part 4: Grinding Stats	85
22.	Update from the Author	92
23.	Chapter 5 Part 1: A Contest of Wits	93
24.	Chapter 5 part 2: A Contest of Wits	98
25.	Chapter 5 Part 3: A Contest of Wits	103
26.	Chapter 5 part 4: A Contest of Wits	109
27.	Chapter 6 Part 1: A Lady's War	114
28.	Chapter 6 Part 2: A Lady's War	119
29.	Chapter 6 Part 3: A Lady's War	123
30.	Chapter 6 Part 4: A Lady's War	128
31.	Doki Doki Magic Love Academy: The Secret Character	133
32.	Chapter 7 Part 1: Life Path Unlocked	137
33.	Chapter 7 Part 2: Life Path Unlocked	142
34.	Chapter 7 Part 3: Life Path Unlocked	148

Chapter 1 Part 1: Academy Bound

"**M**iss!" the maid was calling while running towards me. "Miss, wait!"

Stopping, I turned around and saw Emily, the head maid of "my" father's estate. She was holding a hat with large, ugly ribbons slapping her face as she closed the distance between us.

Gross. I hate hats.

I told Lindsay, my personal maid, and the one now accompanying me to school, not to bother with any more hats. Lindsay protested. It's what all gentile women wear out. You can't go in public without your hat. What would the other nobles think? The shock. The horror. The idiocracy. I remember watching those Victorian movies where the ladies had to wear a bonnet out, but those hats stayed firmly in place the entire duration of their outing. But no. Not these hats. The hats of the Voltare Kingdom were a noble lady's weapon!

Big. Ugly. Uncomfortable. Did I mention ugly?

Here is what I learned about hats. You spend a lot of money to get the ugliest one you can find. Then spend more money adding the gaudiest accessories you can tack on. Make sure it's so heavy you will need a neck brace to actually wear it. Then you wear it out, other ladies compliment or back-hand compliment your hat. Then whoever is the highest-ranking lady, or the lady in charge, or some other social cue I haven't mastered, takes her hat off, then everyone else can too. Then we talk about how to buy more ugly hats, or extra expensive accessories for hats or gossip about someone else's hat.

Did I mention they don't wear their hats for more than five minutes? See before mentioned neck brace part.

Well here comes Emily with the hat my mother made sure had to be extra ugly - perfect - for my arrival at the academy of snobs.

Emily was getting up there in age. I don't know exactly. It's a universal truth to not ask a woman her age. But from what I gathered, she was old enough to have tended to "me" as a baby. 40? Does that sound right? She has a bit of grey coming through her sandy locks and the crinkle of crows feet at her eyes. Hmmmm. Better safe than sorry. I'll say she's 35.

"Miss!" Emily said panting as she caught up with me. "How could you forget your hat?! You must be so nervous."

Not really. Excited? Hell yes. MAGIC! Nervous? Not really. But I didn't want to be rude so I took the disgusting monster from her hands.

"Thank you, Emily," I said with my customer service voice complete with my customer service smile. God, Goddess, or Kami-sama, I really hate retail.

Lindsay takes the hat from me to put it on my head. She's not being very gentle. I think that's her sly way of letting me know that I shouldn't have insisted to go without it. After I acquire 10 lbs more, I head outside to the carriage. My mother is outside snapping last-minute orders to the servants that include ensuring my safety, health, and prospective marriage candidates all in one go.

"Please drive at a moderate speed. Don't let the carriage shake too much. And stay on the main roads. There is absolutely no reason to take a detour. And don't get robbed by bandits! But if you do get robbed by bandits, find the nearest eldest son from a respectable family to save my daughter."

"Mother, if we are being robbed by bandits I would happily accept help from the youngest son of a reputable family!" I tease her.

She gasps as I chuckle. Stupid aristocracy. The younger sons have a hard time. When there is no more land or business to will out, they are left to "make a name for themselves." Which basically means military or church.

"Well, in that case, make sure you ask to meet his older brothers!" She quickly recovers. My mother, Lady Elizabeth Eldergast was still getting used to her daughter's newly formed, playful humor. From what I gathered, the former Christine Eldergast was pretty boring - eh- refined. She spoke when it was needed. Said what was needed. Never had strong opinions and just went with the flow of the situation.

"Naw. They'd already be married." I retort back. Before my mother can get another word in, I quickly take the butler's hand to ascend into the carriage. Why did all those isekai manga's make it seem like the modern girl had such a hard time adapting to rich snob life? To be honest, taking a hand in and out of a carriage was very practical. The dresses had a lot of fluff to navigate. And the step was not that easy either.

"Bye, Mom!" I yell out the door. Which causes another small meltdown. "Mom" is not a lady-like way to address your mother. I did it on purpose.

As soon as the door closes, I hurriedly take off the ugly dead carcass on my head. Let's hit it! It's Hogwarts time!

Chapter 1 Part 2: Academy Bound

Hogwarts! Hogwarts! Hogwarts!

I was chanting in my head over and over.

"We're almost there, miss," Lindsay informs me. I'm practically ready to run the rest of the way there. I can't wait!

The carriage slows down and stops long enough for the driver to give our credentials. We pass through a set of ornate iron gates. I can't see much from my window. Apparently, nobles don't need to see outside as they travel, the window has been buttoned up tightly with curtains. I can only pull away a couple of inches to smash my nose into.

I can see a bit of the grounds. Boring. It's just bushes and grass. I'm sure it's pretty don't get me wrong. But with my limited view, it's not very interesting. I want to see a castle. Or a palace! Or a creepy tower!

The carriage stops. "Miss, you'll be getting off here. I will be taking the rest of your luggage to your room. There should be a Lady Averest waiting to help first years." Lady Averest isn't a person, it's a title. From what I understood, the school selects a Lord and Lady Averest from the 2nd years upon completion of their 1st year. It's a fierce competition. The candidate must have top grades and win a popular vote among the students. In the game, the position of Lady Averest can either be the heroine or the villainess depending on how you played the first year of the game. Since I am neither, there is no reason to stress out about trying to get that position. Regardless of your progression, the Prince always becomes Lord Averest in the 2nd year. Winning the Lady Averest title is part of the requirements to be on the Prince's route since you need to trigger his events while you are performing duties together.

I step out of the carriage into a courtyard and I am.....

Disappointed.

What the hell?!

Why does this school look like a Japanese high school?!

NOOOOOOOOOOOOOOOOOO! You bastard game designers! I forgot this game is a Japanese game. So they always have a little Japanese culture sprinkled in. I want a castle! This is a boring rectangle brick building. I turn around to look at the road the carriage took to come in. Well, the front grounds are pretty basic and much larger than what you would see at a Japanese high school. But still! I feel cheated.

Fine. Hogwarts is just a boring high school. But that will make it easy right? Oh and the classes are what's important. Bring it on Dumbledore!

I head into the inner courtyard where all the activity is centered. HATS! Heh. Heh. I forgot my hat. And Lindsay did too? Wait. Did she?

"Oh, Lady Eldergast!" I turn as I hear someone call my name. Who is this again? I think I met her a couple of weeks ago at a tea party.

Tea parties are the worst. I'm going to avoid them with every fiber of my being.

The unidentified lady glides over to me. I mentally roll my eyes. Gliding isn't a good sign. That usually means villainess.

"Oh my!" she over-reacts. "You've lost your hat!" She is really pumping up the drama here. If this was a cheesy day time soap opera, you would have seen her throw her hand up to her forehead.

"Ahhh," I stammer. "Yes, I sadly left it in the carriage. I was so....." I look around trying to find elegant lady words, "enthralled.... by the grand entrance that I truly lost my wits." Buy it. Buy it. Buy it.

"I see," she deadpans. "I believe Lady Mortia was in a similar stupor. You ought to seak her out!" The other ladies in the entourage start snickering. I was right. Villainess.

Black hair. Green eyes. OH! I remember! This is the villainess. Lady Angelica Baberry.

Abort mission!

"Thank you for your advice, Lady Angelica," I curtsy slightly. Duke Baberry is higher in status than my father Earl Eldergast. So, therefore, Angelica is higher in status than I am. As much as I would like to give this bitch the middle finger and piss off, I can't. As long as I keep my best friend station within the game, and don't stand out too much, I only get sideline bullied. Which compared to what the heroine goes through, isn't bad at all. Keep the peace for now. As long as the heroine doesn't get a bad ending, you'll be long banished and life will be peaceful.

"Well, it IS a shame," she said with an air. "I invited the hatter from.....

And so we start our hat conversation.

Chapter 1 Part 3: Academy Bound

Rose Dorm should be this building?

I stop and stare at the map that was provided. My initial thoughts of this place looking like a Japanese high school was slightly incorrect. Given the size of the academy and that, it also is a boarding school, it more closely resembles a college campus. After passing through the inner courtyard and past the academic buildings, the rest of the academy had the same architectural feel as my home and in town. The dorm buildings looked no different than any grand estate I had visited in my world tour of tea party hell.

Rose Dorm was the building that housed the first-year female students. Even though the Lady Alverest was technically the role model mentor senpai character, she lives in the Pearl Dorm with the other 2nd year female students. Which, in my opinion, doesn't make any sense. Shouldn't she be more available to the first years? But likely this was a result of Game Play. In the game, the Lady Alverest was nothing more than an information character. The heroine has very little do with her unless there was a specific reason like disciplinary actions. During the 2nd year, either the heroine or

Lady Angelica becomes the Lady Alverest so they have to have stupid rivalry stuff happen. That meant they had to stay in close enough proximity to force them together.

I enter Rose Dorm looking around hopelessly. I was given a room assignment, but it was nonsense to me. In America, rooms would be orderly. You would be assigned a number, or letter, or a combination of numbers or letters. My room was listed as The Spring Sage. What does that even mean?

Out of the corner of my eye I see another young girl with pink hair looking around bewildered too. A comrade in arms! If I'm going to be lost, might as well be lost with company!

"Excuse me," I say politely as I grab her attention. "I'm sorry, I'm a bit confused. Do you happen to know which room The Spring Sage is?" Given her perplexed look, I knew she didn't.

"The Spring Sage?" she asked shocked.

Why is she shocked? Oh no. Am I in a weird room? Or the wrong building?!

"Uhhhhhhh," I stammer, "yeah."

"You're Christine Eldergast!!" she suddenly exclaims.

"I....am." Wow, that doesn't sound convincing or ladylike.

"I'm Maria Heroina! We are roommates!"

Maria......Heroina? Heroina? HEROINE! That's right! The heroine's default name is Maria Heroina. I had completely forgotten. The game allows you to input any name you want and I always changed to it my real-life name.

Pink hair. Yellow eyes. Heroine.

Really the pink hair should have clued me in sooner. All the mob characters have fairly normal looking hair. The side characters, like me, might have one distinguishing feature. For me, that would be my "unnatural" purple eyes. But the heroine and capture targets stand out from the crowd.

"Ah, well... it's a pleasure to make your acquaintance." What was the phrase that Japanese always use? It sounds weird translated into English. That's right! I remember. "Please take care of me from now on."

"Please take care of me as well!" she says with a bow.

Maybe I was overthinking my etiquette lessons. Maybe I should use Japanese etiquette and I can make due. This is a Japanese game after all.

"This way!" she grabs my hand. "The dorm is divided into four wings. We are in the Spring hall to the east." She explains with her excitement overflowing. And we start walking down a gaudy - lavishly decorated - hallway. "The decor of this wing is set to envoke a springtime feeling all year round! The mages even enchant the halls to match the sounds and smell of each season. We are lucky we didn't end up in the Winter hall! Everyone complains that it's never warm. The only people who like staying there are the fire mages!"

As we continue walking and round a few corners, Maria is chatting on about the enchantments used in the look of the dorms. I can't pay attention. She wasn't this chatty in the game. Was she? Actually no she wasn't. The heroine was never voiced. The harem of boys did a lot of talking. But that's because they hired well know seiyuu. The heroine's personality can fluctuate based on your decisions and route that you're in. Generally speaking, she will be an honest, nice person. But based on the particular love interest, she will end up spinless or a badass by the end of the game.

"Here we are!" Above the door it has a plaque that says "Sage". Well, I guess the Spring Sage makes sense now.

We walk into the room. It's grander than any dorm room I've ever been in that's for sure. But also, not as grand as my bedroom at the Eldergast estate. There are two moderately sized beds on either side of the room and a desk next to each. In the center, there is a coffee table with sitting chairs to entertain guests.

"□□□!!" Maria exclaims looking around.

Sugoi? Despite this being a Japanese game, has there been any Japanese words? Everything looks and appears in English.

I watch as Maria is prancing around the room. Something doesn't seem right. As she continues to discover the minor magic that is in the room, such as lights that aren't fueled by fire or electricity, she keeps saying sugoi over and over.

"Oh!" Maria suddenly turns her attention back to me. "Do you know what discipline you're aiming for?! Is it light magic? Your brother has light magic, right? I bet it's light magic. You can be a healer! Healers are always needed.

My brother has light magic? I didn't even know that. I guess I sorta remember my father talking offhandedly that Rios' profession was "very respectable." Do I have light magic? I have no idea. Maybe there was an assessment that original Christine Eldergast took and she already knew.

"I suppose," I half-heartedly answer.

"You haven't had an assessment yet?"

"No..." it might be weird for a noble to not have an assessment, but at least I won't have to confidently lie about having a light affinity then turn out to

NOT have a light affinity. "But that's ok." I quickly add. "That's the whole point of going to Hogwarts! So I can figure it out!" I try my best to inject my genuine enthusiasm.

"Hog....warts?" she askes tentativly.

"EH! I mean... The Elverest Academy. Sorry. Dumb nickname I gave to the school. Ignore that."

"Hogwarts? Like, Harry Potter?"

Chapter 1 Part 4: Academy Bound

Harry Potter.

Heh?

HEEEEEEEEEEEEH?!!!!

"Have you been reincarnated too?!" I yell rather loudly and not lady-like.

"Yes! YES! I'm from Japan!" She's shrieking right along with me. "My name is Hamata Yukiko!" She was practically in tears.

"Hi, Yukiko-san," I say starting to break down. "My name is Mackenzie Brown." I can barely say my old name as I start crying. We both hug each other sobbing. I didn't realize how badly I needed to say that. Everything up until now was a dream. That someday I would wake up and find out I was in a coma this whole time. But I said my name out loud. And with someone that, even though lived on the other side of the world as me, understood what it meant.

"Mackenzie-chan!" Maria/Yukiko cried. "We're best friends now."

Pulling our embrace apart to look her in the face, I nod.

"Yes. We are most certainly best friends now!"

After some time of mindless sobbing into each others' shoulders, we calm down enough to sit near the coffee table to talk. Maria and I decided that we are going to use our in-world names since we are now those people. But also agree that our old life names can be used if we needed to relay messages in secret.

I found out that Maria, in her past life, was only a teenager. She died at 17, which makes her the same age as our characters now. She laughed when I told her how I died by truck-kun. Luckily she didn't ask me details. I didn't want to explain the details.

"I played all the routes of Doki Doki Magic Heart Academy! It was my favorite game. I'm so sad I died before the sequel!" Maria told me.

"There was going to be a sequel? I had no idea." I said sipping the herbal tea Lindsay made us to calm down. What a sight for my poor maid. She walked in on two girls, who are essentially strangers, sobbing their eyes out together. We made up some lie about how stressed and scared we were about starting school and were happy and relieved to have found a nice roommate. She brought the tea and I dismissed her so Maria and I could talk about our situation.

"Who was your favorite capture target?!" Maria askes me excitedly.

"Well…..To be honest I only cleared two routes. The game had only just came out."

"It's been out for 5 years though?" she asks puzzled.

"Ah. Well not in America. We have to wait until games like these are translated. And it always takes a long time before we get them."

She makes an O face in comprehension.

"But my favorite isn't important," I lean in expecting to hear some good gossip. "I'm not the heroine. So who are you going to pick?!"

"Oh gosh. I have no idea. I romanced them all in the game!"

"Actually," I sit back up. "Who are the capture targets? I only played Prince Levi's and Sir Grey's routes."

"Sir Grey's bad ending was so sad," she said with a whimper.

"His bad ending?"

"You mean you never saw his bad ending?!"

Now I start feeling guilty. I thought that by playing two routes (I got their good endings) was like half the game and was feeling fairly accomplished. But I just now realized that Japanese otome fans play the WHOLE game. All the targets, both good and bad endings, unlocking secret endings, unlocking secret capture targets. In comparison, I barely scratched the surface.

"I guess I don't know that much."

"That's ok! I will teach you! And you will have to help me pick!"

I nod. Yes, that's a good idea. Maria is both physically and mentally 17 whereas I'm physically 17 but mentally 28. Let this oneesan weed out the bad guys. If I even caught the whiff of a yandere, I'm going to steer well clear of that psychopath.

"I can do that! But first, you need to tell me who we are looking out for."

"Right!"

Doki Doki Magic Love Academy: The Prince

P rince Levi Alistar Sunspire

Appearance: short blond hair, bright blue eyes.

Age: 17

Blood Type: AB

Why is this important?

"It's very important!"

But I never understand why Japanese games include blood type.

"It's like your horoscope."

So what does AB mean?

"I guess talented and composed."

Huh. Ok.

Magical Affinity: fire combat

Oh, that's right. In your 2nd year you either specialize in magical combat or spell casting.

"Stop interrupting."

:(

Back Story:

Prince Levi is the 2nd son of King Alfonse Rubia Sunspire and Queen Elina Sunspire. He is the crown prince, surpassing his brother.

Why?

"Let me finish!"

Prince Levi's older brother was an unreliable, obnoxious flirt. He never took anything seriously and eventually ran off. When he didn't return for 3 years, the King had enough and removed him from the line of succession. His current whereabouts are unknown.

"But it's rumored he will be in Doki Doki Magic Love Academy 2!"

Wait isn't he older?

"Yeah, so?"

Why would he be going to school in the sequel?

"It probably won't take place in school."

Then how can they call it Doki Doki Love Academy if there is no Academy?!

shrugs

For Prince Levi's route you will need --

I

"What?"

You're the heroine. You should say I will need.

"Fine."

For Prince Levi's route, I will need to perfect my grades and win the popular vote to become the Lady Alverest. I will also need to choose water as my affinity.

You get to choose?!

"In the game, yes. But to be honest, I don't know if I will be able to choose in real life."

Oh. Will that hurt your prospects?

"Maybe a little for some of the targets. But you can choose a different affinity. The capture targets will just start with a lower romance stat. I thought you said you played Prince Levi's route."

I did, but I just randomly did stuff and ended up with him at the end.

"...."

In Prince Levi's good ending, after he defends me against Lady Angelica and we banish her from the kingdom, he will ask for my hand in marriage.

Yeah, I thought it was a pretty boring ending.

"It kinda is. Pretty safe."

In Prince Levi's bad ending, Lady Angelica convinces everyone I was in league with the Rubar Kingdom in a secret assassination plot and I am killed at the end of year ball.

Wait, what?! Killed??

"Yeah."

Oh my god, I am definitely NOT letting you romance the prince. Not even taking that chance.

Doki Doki Magic Love Academy: The Knight

S ir Adrian Grey

Appearance: short black hair, grey eyes.

Totally my type!

Age: 20

Blood Type: A

What does that mean?

"stressed and conscientious"

That makes no sense.

"No less than being a Virgo or Leo does!"

Magic Affinity: Air Combat

Back Story: Sir Grey is Prince Levi's personal guard. A prodigy with the sword, he is expected to someday take over the command of the Kingdom's military. Likely when Prince Levi takes the crown. He is the youngest of 3 brothers -

My mother wouldn't like him.

"Why?"

He doesn't have property or business. A sad younger son.

"But he's going to be super important."

Not like I can convince her of that!

"True. Anyways..."

He is the youngest of 3 brothers and has one younger sister. In most of the routes, you learn very little about him since he mostly acts in support of Prince Levi. However, in his personal route, you find out he's a major sis-con.

Right! I remember having to help him buy gifts to send home! She's like 5 right?

"Yeah. There's a 15 year age gap between them."

Something doesn't seem right about that.

"There are fan theories online that she might be HIS child."

WHAT?!

"I know!"

For Sir Grey's route, I will have to pick combat magic. The exact affinity isn't important as long as I can enroll in the combat classes.

Right! I picked wind, same as him, and had to raise my sword and tactical stats SO much.

"I hated how much you had to play Combat Wizards to level your tactical skill!"

Hahaha. I know! And what was annoying is that the minigame was lame too.

"Yeah, it wasn't fun."

In Sir Grey's good ending, it basically follows Prince Levi's route but slightly different. I help dismantle the assassination plot and expose Lady Angelica at the same time. There's a pretty intense battle leading up to the end of year ball where the dramatic reveal happens. It also ends with an engagement.

Lady Angelica is killed this time.

"Yeah, they had evidence of her involvement."

In Sir Grey's bad ending, you fail to uncover the whole plot in time. Sir Grey's family is taken hostage. He decides to fulfill his duty and without your help, is not able to save his family in time. His entire family, including the sister, is killed. He inherits his family estate, but he is completely destroyed as a man.

His family is murdered!? That's horrible.

"Yeah, it was so sad. Especially since his whole route he gushes about his sister."

Regardless of romance choice, you need to save his family!

"Maybe YOU should save his family."

Why me?

snickers "You said he's your type."

B-but I'm NOT the heroine!

"I'm not going to aim for a full harem ending. There is plenty to share!"

Doki Doki Magic Love Academy: The Wizard

Lord Simon Clark

Appearance: long midnight blue hair, usually in a loose side braid. dark green eyes.

Age: 18

Blood Type: B

"Practical and relaxed"

I'm glad you knew I was going to ask.

"Naturally."

Magical Affinity: dual water and fire spell caster

That sounds pretty powerful.

"He is. Actually Lord Simon can wield all the disciplines fairly well, but the affinities are where he is the strongest. While dual affinity isn't super rare, the two elements being opposite of each other is."

How so?

"I didn't really understand in the game. I guess maybe now we are in school we will find out why."

Ah.

Back story: Lord Simon starts the game already in his 2nd year.

The game takes place over 2 years. How does he end up hanging out for the entirety of next year?

"There are some milestones you have to achieve. I guess I'll tell you that before the back story."

In order to get Lord Simon to stay when you enter your 2nd year, you have to have a high enough romance level with him and trigger his career flag.

Career flag?

"Yeah. Currently, he easily masters all the magic he learns so he doesn't have any goals or plans for the rest of his life. If you don't trigger an event that helps him decide on a career, he won't stay."

I see. But how does picking a career make him stay?

"He decides he needs to learn more and signs on to take private tutoring for an additional year. It's strongly implied this is also to stay close to the heroine."

Which is you.

"Yes. To stay close to me. Anyways..."

Back story continued: Marquess David Clark is Simon's father. Simon is the eldest son and is expected to inherit after his father. You find out in his route his mother is already dead. Marquess Clark has been pressuring

Simon to marry early since he doesn't have any siblings and he is worried about succession should something happen.

It's common for nobility to need back up heirs, I suppose.

"Even with healing magic taking care of most minor injuries and illnesses, there still is war and general violence."

In addition to gaining a high enough romance level and triggering the career flag, I will need to specialize in any affinity spellcasting, except for light magic.

Why not light magic?

"There's another character that completely dominates your time if you end up as a light caster. So there isn't any room for Lord Simon to make a move."

Oh god. It isn't a yandere?

"No, nothing like that. I'll get to him next."

To get Simon's good ending, I will have to help him with his magical research which involves collecting a lot of random items. Some of these items are a once time catch, so if you miss the chance to acquire it you will not make it to the good ending. He will also propose at the end of year ball.

That sounds hard.

"He has a pretty difficult route. The romance level in the first year is hard enough. Then the item collection has to start before you even know about the quest."

So in his case, it's easier to get a bad ending.

"Yep. Although his bad ending isn't as bad as some of the others."

Simon's bad ending will trigger if you fail to collect all of the required items. His magical experiment will fail and he will return home. Since he feels the additional year of study didn't achieve anything, he will enter a marriage proposal with Lady Angelica to appease his father.

Awww. I wouldn't wish anyone a life with her. Wait... does she even show up in his route?

"Actually no. She is never interested in him. I guess his route is hard enough so they decided not to have her make it harder."

A small blessing. But that means they both end up marrying someone they don't have any interest in.

"Seems like it."

That does sound like a bad ending.

Doki Doki Magic Love Academy: The Professor

P rofessor Alan McGreggor

Hold up a minute. A professor? Like one of our teachers?

"Yeah."

HOW OLD IS HE!?

Appearance: messy shoulder-length brown hair. sometimes kept as a low ponytail. brown eyes.

How. Old.

Age: 30

NO!

"Huh?"

No! You're not dating him!

"Eh....why?"

He's too old! That should be illegal. Wait! It IS illegal! You're a minor. Is he a creepy pedophile?!

"Actually in the game you can legally get married at 15."

Doesn't matter. No. No. Hard pass, no!

"Can I continue?"

Sure. But it's still no.

Blood type: A

Magical Affinity: light magic healer

No way! He's the reason Lord Simon can't romance you if you chose a light magic discipline?

"Yes, because he's your teacher. You will spend all your time with him."

I hate him.

"...."

Back story: Professor McGreggor is one of the kingdom's most talented healers. He served in the war with the Rubar Kingdom with King Sunspire. However, having experienced the tragedy of war, he struggled with even the most basic healing spells when get got home. He eventually was able to perform the lowest level of healing but never fully recovered. So he teaches here at the academy.

In order to get his good ending....

....

What?

"You're not going to interrupt me?"

It doesn't matter. You won't be romancing him.

"...."

In order to get his good ending, I will need to obviously choose light magic as my affinity. The route is pretty straight forward as I will need to continue to volunteer to have additional tutoring or assist with any healing related requests. Eventually, he admires my dedication to helping people and it heals his wounded heart. After a kidnapping event where I am gravely injured, he is able to use his healing magic again. He proposes after saving you.

No end of year ball?

"No. The kidnapping takes place at the same time."

In the bad ending, if your romance level wasn't fully maxed out, Professor McGreggor won't have it in him to perform the higher level healing magic and the heroine dies from her wounds.

WHAT?! Death?!

"Yes."

Yeah no. You are so not getting close to him. If you end up with light magic, you better pack your bags and leave town.

Doki Doki Magic Love Academy: The Aristocrat

Duke Victor Mossgrave

Duke?

"I'll get to that."

Appearance: short red hair. silver eyes.

Age: 17

Same year as us?

"Yes."

Blood Type: O

"energetic and social"

I actually don't even care about this anymore.

Magical Affinity: Water spell casting

So why is he a duke?

Back story: His father the late Duke Mossgrave died during the war with Rubar. Victor was only 7 when his father died and inherited the title. His mother, Dutchess Oliva Mossgrave and Victor's uncle on his mother's side Earl Fairvilla has been running the estate until Victor completed school to take over. In his route, you learn that his uncle is abusing the power and is bleeding the Mossgrave estate dry.

Why am I not surprised by that?

"What do you mean?"

I guess what I'm saying is that it's not a very original plot point; the relative stealing from the too young lord.

"I suppose. But I wouldn't call any of these routes very original."

Very true. But I feel like I know what his route consists of. Revenge?

"Yeah basically. Oh, I forgot to mention..."

Duke Victor is a notorious playboy.

Ugghhhh. These last couple of capture targets are the worst.

In order to get his good ending, you will have to max out your charisma level.

How the hell do you do that?

"Lots of tea parties."

Gross!

To get his good ending, I will have to let Lady Angelica win the Lady Alverest position. Angelica will abuse her position to bully me and assign me detention work. Duke Victor will see similarities in the abuse of power and we will be comrades in arms to not only expose Angelica but allow

Victor to take his estate back over. I will be the first woman he sees as an equal which makes him lose interest in all the other ladies.

I'm disgusted about how cliche this is. Lemme guess. He proposes at the end of year ball.

"Yep."

In his bad ending, if I fail to max out my charisma or end up as the Lady Alverest, Victor will not see me as an equal. His route will play through almost the same as the good ending but instead of a marriage proposal, you catch him cheating on you with Lady Angelica.

Figures. But it's not really that bad of an ending.

"Not really. But the challenging part is that you might not know if you maxed out your charisma. It's a hidden stat in the game."

Well, it's hidden in real life too. Might not be worth romancing him, the tea parties alone aren't worth it.

"I like tea parties."

Gasp! That breaks my heart.

Chapter 2 Part 1: The Game Begins

Man, I'm tired.

Maria and I stayed up entirely too long talking about the capture targets and our mutual reincarnation. Since Maria played through the game to 100% completion, she knew a lot about the story. What had us both nervous was how our reincarnation was going to affect it. Will the story continue with its predetermined route or will we drastically alter it simply by being different people? We decided on a few things we felt wouldn't change.

1. The personalities of the capture targets. Neither of us have meet any of the capture targets prior to starting the academy. Their personality was unlikely to deviate from the game. But we did agree that a real person is more complex than a game character, so we are ready for some surprises.

2. The assassination plot seemed to play a common thread in a few routes. It also proceeded without notice for the majority of the routes it was in until the heroine and capture target start finding evidence. We both felt that the assassination plot will still be present, but how severe it becomes

will be unknown. In my opinion, Lady Angelica is the deciding factor. In Prince Levi and Sir Grey's route, she was directly or indirectly implied to have helped. But in the other routes, she didn't seem involved and there wasn't any mention of the assassination attempt. My theory is that her help moves the plot along, and her inaction causes it to be squashed.

3. Maria's choice may not be a choice. Gameplay for otome games depends heavily on player choice. Which stats do you level? What affinity do you pick? Which location do you visit to trigger events with certain characters? But real life doesn't have the same freedoms a game does. We both doubt Maria will have absolute choice on her magical affinity. No one does. And there is no real-life meter of game stats. Someone like Lord Simon requires a high romance stat or Sir Grey who requires tactical stats. We will have no what of knowing if we are hitting those benchmarks. And we might not even be able to. Even if I play Combat Wizards day and night, would I actually have the tactical prowess to impress Sir Grey?

It is nerve-racking. But as it is too soon to tell, all we can do is focus on our first day.

Maria and I both got ready and wore our new school uniforms. Despite the dresses that I wore at home being so big and fluffy, the school uniforms were far more practical. First-year students' uniforms are black and white, indicating no particular magical affinity or discipline. The second-year students however have a rainbow of colors. For example, the fire students have red and white uniforms. If you are fire combat, the uniform is dark red and if you are fire spell casting, then the uniform is a softer red (almost looks pink to me, but don't say that to any of the fire kids). Maria and I are both wearing a white blouse with the school insignia embroidered on the left. Ladies wore a black ribbon tied at the collar while the boys wore ties. Our uniforms had black circle skirts that stop at mid-shin where our boots met. Later in the year when it gets colder, we have a sweater to wear over the blouse. I'm a little upset the women don't get suit jackets whereas the boys do. Our version of the uniform looks so plain. That jacket really does make it real snazzy.

After eating a quick breakfast in our room courtesy of Lindsay and Julie - Julie is Maria's maid - we made our way to the school's auditorium.

"This is where the game starts!" Maria said in a low tremble. Was it excitement or fear? Maybe it was both.

"Right. The tutorial." I look at her. "What is the tutorial again?"

"The headmaster explains the history and disciplines of the school. Then at towards the end he talks about the first years finding their affinity and how to test for it. All the first years will be tested throughout the year, and some may not find their affinities right away."

"Oh, that's right! I remember in the game this is when you select your affinity."

"Yeah. I'm pretty nervous about that."

"Because you don't know if you will be able to choose."

"Not only that," she adds, "but when I am randomly chosen, the headmaster assumed it wouldn't come up with anything. It's supposed to assure the first years that it might take a while. But in the game, the heroine lights up right away and everyone acts shocked. The teachers will give her special treatment and that's part of the reason Lady Angelica targets the heroine."

"Ooooooooh," I say as we take our seats. I hadn't thought about it from a practical standpoint. Picking the magical affinity was just a prompt on the screen. To be honest, I never paid that much attention to reactions after doing so. Yes, I'm special. Yes, I'm the heroine. Let's move on. But Maria is about to live that moment.

"You got this," I say reassuring her. "Afterall, I'm your best friend!"

She looks at me with a giant smile on her face. I'm glad I can say that and mean it. I hadn't actually thought about whether I would even like the heroine. But since she also has been reincarnated, it really wasn't hard to have an instant bond. That's right. My job is to support the heroine! I'll make sure these real-life capture targets aren't shitty men (like that Professor!) and help make sure she gets a happy ending!

Chapter 2 Part 2: The Game Begins

I watch as Maria nervously stands on the stage. Just as we thought, she was "randomly" picked from the first-year students to demonstrate how magical affinity testing worked. This may sound terrible, but the 28-year-old American college graduate just couldn't sit through the headmaster's speech. Not only was he monotoned, but he had a metronomic speaking pace. Everything blurred together into one uninterrupted sentence that a few minutes in, I had completely lost focus. A couple of times I had peaked at Maria and she looked like she was listening intently. Maybe it was because Japanese teenagers were more studious than Americans or maybe it was because she was living her personal fantasy, but I just don't know how she did it. Oh well. I'll get the cliff notes explanation from her later.

What kind of person am I? Mentally I'm 11 years older than her and yet on day one, I already have to ask her for class notes.

"To explain how the magical affinity testing works, may I present Thea Tutorial, The Lady Averest," the headmaster droned.

Thea.....Tutorial. Tutorial?! No way! Her NAME is Tutorial?!

I'm laughing.

I'm laughing so hard I'm in tears. It catches the attention of everyone sitting nearby, but I just can't stop.

Tutorial!

Maria's name is LITERALLY Heroine... Heronia.

Maria is starting at me laughing and she starts snickering too. She caught it too. Oh, thank god. We are going to have a good time with this!

"Welcome to The Alverest Magic Academy for the Elite!" The - I mean - Lady Tutorial says. "Students upon completion of your first year at the academy will be identified with one of the magical affinities. Additionally, you will specialize in either combat or spell casting. Combat is --"

My mind starts to wander. I'm sure if I had the game script in front of me, her speech is likely word for word. But I didn't pay attention to the Tutorial chapter. I start to look at the people in the hall. I wonder if I can find any of the capture targets? They all should be here.

I turn around and notice a boy with bright red hair a couple of rows back with a girl snuggled into either arm. He catches my eye and makes a cheeky grin, which I visibly disgust at and quickly turn around. He kinda stood out a bit. My mind is going through the rolodex of information Maria recited last night. Who had red hair again? Not the Prince or Sir Grey for sure. He's a student so not that slimy professor. Oh! The playboy duke with a revenge plot. Victor....something. I take a peek back, and he's staring right at me and makes a little wave. Tsk.

Glancing towards the sides of the hall I notice a very well built man standing by one of the closed doors of the west exit. He has an almost intimidating aura about him and simply looking at him sent a little shiver down my spine. He must be a guard or something. Even though he is a bit far away, it almost looks like his eyes are glowing red. Ok. That's pretty scary and I turn back to the stage.

Maybe looking for capture targets isn't a good idea right now.

Focus on Maria. That's my job.

"....if you don't successfully find your affinity the first time. As you refine your magical talents, your affinity will naturally come to you." The tutorial had continued on.

"Now Lady Maria, please place your hand over the affinity stone." Affinity stone? Are there six? Do I have to make sure Thanos doesn't get this one? Haha. I crack myself up.

I start laughing again. Although the death glares I receive this time snuffs out my laughter pretty quickly.

Maria cautiously places her hand over the jet black ball. It kinda looks like a bowling ball. But one of those pretty bowling balls that has the fancy glitter swirl pattern.

I lean forward in my seat. What will she get?! Now I'm excited and my heart is pounding in my ears.

The bowling affinity ball starts to light up and glows a radiant blue color causing gasps in the audience.

"WATER MAGIC?!" someone screams from the crowd.

The room erupts with chatter. And my mind is spinning.

Ok. Water. Capture targets. Who does this benefit? Think. Think.

The Prince! I chose water magic on my first playthrough not caring about any decision in particular. And I remember Maria mentioning that since he is fire, the heroine needs to choose water. The Prince isn't a bad choice, but the assassination plot does come into play.

Who else?

Sir Grey. But only if Maria leans towards combat and tactical. While I will be sad to let my bias go, he also is a good choice. The assassination plot is still in play AND we need to save the sister.

Lord Simon. Again any element other than light, with a spellcasting focus. Solid choice, however, his requirements might be too high.

Duke Victor Playboy. Maria said water spellcasting, although I don't know why. Thinking back on the redhead I saw earlier, he is not a solid choice.

Wait a second. This doesn't really eliminate --

I stop mid-thought.

No, it does!

It eliminates the pedophile teacher!

"Yeeeeeeeeeees!" I accidentally cheer out loud.

Chapter 2 Part 3: The Game Begins

The crowd was too dense. After the chaotic ending of the tutori - er - the entrance ceremony, the students had spilled out to the common areas. I haven't been able to find Maria. If I had to guess using my game knowledge, Maria is currently getting a tour of the campus explaining where all the activities are located. I pout inwardly to myself. I wanted a tour. But in the game, the tour was for the heroine and her best friend certainly didn't tag along.

I was shuffling along lost in thought when I nearly walked straight into a student.

"What the?" I gasp as I come to my senses. I look up and see a wide smile and red hair.

Red alert! Red alert! An alarm was blaring in my head. Shiiiiiiiiiiit. Isn't this -

"Why, hello my sweet chickadee!" he swoops in gracefully to take my hand and land a light kiss.

My modern American sensibilities react automatically and I jerk my hand away, wiping the top of my hand that was slightly wet on my skirt.

"Hi. Bye." I say quickly as I attempt to step around him. He quickly matches my move and remains in front of me.

"Well I was hoping to wait until a ball, but if you would like to dance, it would be to my absolute pleasure," he coos.

I make a very unladylike noise from the back of my throat. Wow. Do men like this really exist? Wait. Dumb question. I'm in otome game land. Yes, men like this exist. How do I answer him? Mackenzie Brown wants to kick him and tell him to stop being a disgusting skirt chaser. But he also is one of Maria's capture targets and I shouldn't ruin her chances by picking a fight with one of them. And he does relinquish his playboy ways once he falls in love with the heroine. Fine. I'll play nice.

"Forgive me, Your Grace," I say emphasizing that I'm fully aware of who he is, even if I don't remember his full name. "I'm afraid I'm a bit out of sorts from the excitement of this morning's ceremony and I'm not in the right state of mind to have an official meeting. If you would like to make arrangements with my maid, I can certainly find time at a later date to make your acquaintance."

"Well my lady," his voice also changing to something more closely resembling what a gentile noble should sound like. "I shall certainly take you up on your offer. Please don't allow me to take up any more of your time and rest well." He gives me a slight bow and steps to the side.

I curtsy slightly in return and take this opportunity to make my escape. I slap my cheeks slightly. Stay away from the capture targets, dummy!

I never said this out loud to Maria, but I am slightly worried about my relationship with the boys. The best friend in the game is a side character. She supports Maria and does very little. But I've read a ton of those isekai reincarnation stories where the protagonist shifts to whoever the main character is, regardless of what their original role was within the story. If Maria was a mindless NPC, then maybe I would have a little fun and romance the harem. But Maria is also a reincarnater like myself. And she loves this game. This is her fantasy. And double and, she is only 17 and never had a real romance before. I'm 28. I've had boyfriends and I don't need to be seducing kids 10 years younger than me.

I should have headed to Rose dorm, but in truth I was a bit lost. The crowd has pushed me along before I was able to break free, I walked around without paying attention, and now I'm half running away from a playboy. Something catches my eye. I stop and stare for a moment.

COMBAT WIZARDS!

I'm in the combat gardens. I don't know the real name of this location. But this garden is where the 2nd year combat students typically hang out. It's one of the few areas I know since I worked so hard to romance Sir Grey. Did I like the Combat Wizards mini game? Absolutely not. But I did get really good at it since I had to play so much of it.

I prance over to where the game tables are. The mini-game was a strategy game for two players. They would have an army of wizards on a grid playing field. The pieces moved and fought based on a hand of cards. Each player starts with 20 cards, 10 of which are the same between both players and 10 of which are randomly chosen. Looking at the table set up, it looks nearly identical to the gameplay screen during the minigame.

There arn't many students here right now so I sit down at one of the empty tables staring intently at the board.

"Do you want to play?" a voice says from behind me.

"Yes!" I reply without looking up.

He sits down across from me and presses his hand to the table bringing his side of the battlefield to life. I copy his motion and my side lights up as well. This minigame sucked. I never liked it. But why is it that now it's in front of me I can't help but get excited.

The game board, which now looks like an LCD screen to my surprise, deals out the cards. It's touch screen! It's EXACTLY like the minigame. Here I thought I was going to have to hold physical cards.

I'm laughing like a villainess about to land a killing bow on a helpless victim. I'm going to destroy this kid!

"You can go first." He says.

I look up at my opponent for the first time and the blood drains from my face.

"SIR GREY?!"

Chapter 2 Part 4: The Game Begins

"Eat fireballs!"

"While a valiant effort, your final act of desperation will not save you from defeat," Sir Grey says calmly.

I'm very annoyed! After I got over my initial panic of suddenly playing Combat Wizards with the man himself, I had already made several critical errors that swung the game considerably in his favor. He was right, I was desperate. Desperately in love. I cringe at my inner thoughts. Even my own jokes are not saving me from humiliation.

Sir Grey was incredibly good looking. Since he was a couple of years older than the students here, he didn't have that baby face college freshman look about him that I saw with Duke Playboy. I really wanted to stare at him more, but the game was requiring too much of my focus.

After playing my hand, I let out an audible sigh. We both knew he would defeat me with his turn, so it was just a matter of watching the hand play out.

"Strangle thorn is active this turn and with that, I take your last wizard."

"I graciously die, "I chuckle slightly as I lean back in my chair.

"If this was a real battle I would consider taking you hostage. Skilled enemies can often become valuable turncoats."

Laughing slightly I say, "You would have me become a spy?"

"It would be a generous offer."

"Luckily I have no pride to wound, so I'm happy to be your 007."

"007?"

"Eh..." Crap, I forgot to act like a noble lady. "007 was a spy in a.... uh... novel that I read a long time ago. That was his code name."

"Interesting." The conversation falls flat as Sir Grey has nothing left to add.

I remember the game being like this too. The initial interactions with Sir Grey were a struggle to get through since he wouldn't talk much past what was required. Part of me really wants to ask about his sister to see what kind of reaction I would get. But I remind myself that Maria has yet to make her choice and I do want to shake up the story too much until she settles in. But, ho ho, Sir Grey, if Maria doesn't choose you, I'm going to swoop in for the kill!

Since I know this is the natural end of this particular conversation, it's best I flex my mental maturity and wrap things up.

"Thank you, Sir Grey for the game. Perhaps with some practice, I might be able to attain a level in which you may find a rematch challenging," I say as I rise from the chair.

Sir Grey stands as well and gives me a bow. "It would be my pleasure to entertain a rematch and I look forward to seeing your progress."

"Peaceful blessings to you, sir." I use the Voltare Kingdom's greeting that was drilled into my etiquette training. As I turn to leave I suddenly remember. I still don't know where I am. But I don't want to pester Sir Grey anymore so I start walking like I know where I am going.

Game knowledge is not helping with actually getting around. The game didn't have an actual map. The map screen was just a bunch of icons that you would highlight and fast travel too. Why didn't we get a map? We should have gotten a map.

My stomach started growling towards the end of our game reminding me I had only a light breakfast several hours ago. I make food my next priority. I know the academy has a dining hall since that was one of the fast travel locations that some events would take place. I miss my cell phone. I wish I could text Maria to meet me for lunch. In any case, I am done wandering around aimlessly, so I need to ask someone for directions. Looking around as the people around me I quickly rule out asking any other first-year student. They have more of a chance to not know the campus as well either. I scan the area for any 2nd-year students.

I see someone in a light blue 2nd year coat. If I remember correctly, that means he's a water spellcaster. I walk up to him with purpose and tap his should to get his attention.

"I'm very sorry to disturb you. But I was wondering if you could point me in the direction of the dining hall?"

He turns towards me with a quizzical look on his face. "The dining hall?" he asks. But I get the sense he isn't asking the question because he questioned where I wanted to go but more because he was questioning why I wanted to go.

"Ah, well you see I missed lunch as I got sidetracked with a game of Combat Wizards. And I'm a first-year, so I am a bit lost."

"This way," he says and starts walking.

"You don't have to escort me there!" I say feeling a little guilty. "I don't wish to hold you up so I just getting directions would be enough."

"I think I need to eat too," he says.

"You think?" How does someone not know if they are hungry?

"I don't think I ate today," he says almost as if he's questioning if what he was saying was correct.

"Well then, you probably should eat if you can't remember!" I say with fake enthusiasm. If he has an eating disorder, I need to encourage eating. "If you'd like, we can eat together. I only have one friend here and I lost track of her after the entrance ceremony. And meals always taste better with others!"

"They do?" he asks quietly.

"Of course! Pardon my manners. I am Christine Eldergast, daughter of Earl Eldergast."

"Simon."

"Pardon?" I can barely hear him speak. Is he shy? Maybe suddenly speaking to a stranger is really hard for him.

"I'm Simon Clark, son of Marquess Clark."

"Nice to make your acquaintance Lord Simon!"

Hold up a moment.

Simon?

Noooooooooooooo! He's another capture target!!

Why is my luck like this?! Maria, I'm sorry I'm not trying to steal your harem I swear!

We walk in silence for the rest of the way to the dining hall. I lost all will power to keep a conversation flowing and Lord Simon wasn't making any attempts either. He stops just slightly inside the hall as if confused by what he was seeing. We stand there silently for an uncomfortable moment.

"Lord Simon?" I ask politely to get his attention. "This is my first time here. How does it work? Is there a place to order? Or do we just sit down?"

He looks at me with a blank expression. "We sit."

"Ok...... Where would you like to sit?"

The stares at me with no answer.

"Ah heh," I say nervously, "I can pick. Let's go over there," I point towards a quiet corner. There arn't many students here right now, but considering how difficult this is for him, I have a feeling he would feel at ease away from the action.

I direct him to a table and we take a seat.

"Why this one?" he asks.

"What do you mean?"

"Why this table. It has four chairs. That table," he says pointing, "has two chairs. So why this one and not that one?"

BECAUSE WE ARE NOT ON A DATE! I mentally scream at him.

"I dislike small tables. When the food comes out they get crowded and I don't like that," I lie.

"You don't like being crowded."

"Uh...not in general," I say with hesitation.

A waiter comes to the table with menus. I quickly assess that the dining hall operates like a restaurant. After reading over the menu, I decide on a chicken dish.

"Is it good?" he asks me ignoring the waiter looking at him.

"I don't know. I've never had it before."

"Then why did you order it if you don't know if you will like it?"

"Well, it seems like something I would like. I read the description and it has many things I know I like, so I am taking the risk of trying it."

"I see," he says looking intently at the menu. "I will try it too."

"Are you sure?" I ask as the waiter collects the menus and leaves with our order.

"You are uncertain of the meal. So I should evaluate it too."

He's so strange.

I never played his route in Doki Doki Magic Love Academy so I only know the information Maria told me. Which I am now realising didn't include any basic information about their personalities. Lord Simon is shy and quiet. And he completely doesn't understand social cues. But Maria said he was basically a magical prodigy. Maybe he's on the spectrum? Somehow I can't imagine the game devs being proactive about representation. So this must be what happens when a 2D character is suddenly fleshed out into a real person.

"Christine!!" I hear someone calling my name so I scan the room for where the voice came from.

"Oh! Maria!" I yell waving my arms to beckon her over. She does a slight jog to make her way over to our table. She sits down next to me and gives me a big hug.

"I'm so sorry I couldn't find you!"

"That's ok," I say patting her head. I notice Lord Simon watching our interaction silently. Great timing, Maria! "Ah, sorry Lord Simon," I say pushing Maria off me gently. "This is my friend I told you about, Maria Heroina. Maria, may I introduce Lord Simon Clark."

I watch her eyes get big as she stares at the man across from us.

"I'm so sorry!" she says suddenly. "I am Maria Heroina, daughter of Baron Heroina."

"I am Simon Clark," he says leaving out the rest of the introduction. Maybe there's more to Marquess Clark wanting him to marry early.

"Do.... do you know each other?" she asks. I know the tone she is using really means, how did you end up together?

"We just made each other acquaintance. I was lost and asked Lord Simon for directions to the dining hall. I was - uh - luckily Lord Simon was also hungry and we decided to eat together. Doyouwannajoin us?" My question came out faster than I meant it to. I was a little panicked now that he was here. "Uh, if that's alright with you, Lord Simon."

"Yes," he says without pleasantries.

"I ate already. But I am happy to get dessert!" Maria says excitedly.

Thank goodness. The meal with Lord Simon alone would have been challenging, but now that Maria is here, she can use her heroine powers on Lord Simon and I can sit back and enjoy the show. Finally something went right today.

Chapter 3 Part 1: Of Magic and Men

"You're kidding!" Maria exclaims in disbelief.

After our late lunch, we both couldn't wait to sneak back to our dorm room to speak freely about what happened today. Lunch was also mentally exhausting for me. Despite my best efforts to keep Lord Simon included in the conversation, he would so little that it would grind any topic to a halt.

"I know! I was so taken off guard I completely bombed my game!" I say after taking a sip of my tea. Tea really is the perfect drink for gossiping. Maybe this is the real reason for all those tea parties.

"But in the game, the first time you are able to play Sir Grey isn't until after raising your strategy to level 7."

"But I'm not you. Maybe I don't need the same requirements as you."

"I suppose," Maria says sounding not entirely convinced.

"Look. Wouldn't it be weird if he wouldn't play ANYONE until they were a certain level? And how does he even judge that? I doubt any of the capture targets can secretly see imaginary stats about us."

"There has to be a way....they just know."

I shrug my shoulders. Truth is what do we even know? It's still much too early to have an idea of how our presence is affecting the game.

"Anyways....." she continues. "You met three capture targets today! I haven't even met one!"

"But you got to learn about the cool features of the academy!"

Maria had filled me in on what I missed. After the entrance ceremony ended, the headmaster had made Lady Tutorial.... I can't even think her name without laughing.... give Maria a tour of the campus. Most of what Maria said wasn't all that surprising except for the message system. In the game, when you got a message, it looked very similar to getting an email notification. There was an envelope looking icon and a little alert would be on it letting you know you had a message. I assumed we would just get handwritten letters. But, just like how I was surprised Combat Wizards looked identical to the mini-game and played on a touchscreen, the mail also had surprising digital elements.

In designated areas on campus and in the common areas of the dorms, there were tables with those touchscreens embedded in them. The mail system worked the same as in the game. Maria told me the touch screens were called rainbow glass here in the game world. I guess to create rainbow glass required the coordinated work of both a fire spellcaster and a water spellcaster. I'm also wondering if the game devs had some biases to water and fire users. We haven't even started our first day and I am hearing about water and fire magic non-stop and haven't even heard a peep about wind, blossom, light, or shadow.

Side note about the blossom users, Maria has shared some Japanese insight with me. In the English version of the game, they had translated the magic to "blossom." But in the original Japanese version of the game, the school of magic was called Hanasakuya, which is derived in part from the Japanese goddess of "delicate earthly life's" name. I guess it just didn't hold up to western translation.

"That wasn't all that fun. I've seen the tutorial 13 times."

"Why thirteen?"

"Six capture targets with two endings each, plus the full harem ending."

"Six capture targets?" I say as I silently count down the ones she had told me about.

"Oh, yeah there's six. There's a hidden character too."

"Hidden character?! Why didn't you tell me about him? Who is he?"

Maria hesitates a moment before answering. "I don't think we will see him, so we shouldn't need to worry about him."

"What do you mean he isn't going to show up? Isn't he already here?"

"Well in order to unlock him, you had to have beat one route first. Then, starting on the 2nd playthrough, the secret character appears if you visit the right places on very specific days. He's not a student, so initial interactions are really important to lure him to visit the school more often."

I start intently at Maria trying to read her mind. She's holding back something. Up until now, she has happily over explained everything. "What are you not saying, Maria?" I ask out loud.

She sighs. "I don't like him."

"Really?"

"Yes," she sighs again. "I love this game and all the characters! But the secret character..... I just don't like him."

Maybe he's a yandere and that's why she's not saying anything. I stare more hoping I have some mental power of persuasion to get her to spill the details, but it seems she has great immunity to my make-believe power and remains silent on the matter.

"Fine. Keep your secrets. I guess we just have to focus on who we have already. Having successfully saved you from the creepy pedophile, we don't need to add another unworthy man to the mix."

I see Maria rolling her eyes. "Professor McGreggor is a perfectly fine romance target."

"No he isn't and good riddance. Anyways....." I say trying to change topics before we fight about this more. "Is there anything noteworthy happening tomorrow?"

"Hmmmm....." Maria ponders. "Lady Angelica is introduced tomorrow. We have a few classes together and she starts to say mean things to me. And...." I can tell she's thinking hard. "I'm pretty sure I meet all the capture targets tomorrow too."

"Heh?! Really?"

"Yeah. It's one of the weakest moments in the game. I think they couldn't figure out how to write them all into one spot very well so it's super awkward."

"This should be fun to watch!"

"You won't be there," Maria deadpans.

"No! Why?!"

"I'll be asked to go to the headmaster's office. They will all be there for some reason or another."

"I have to spend the day without you again!" I say with a pout. Maria reaches over and pats my head. Well, at least I won't run into any capture targets then if they are all together for Maria's first day. Maybe I should have more of a plan of what to do tomorrow. Oooooo, maybe I should see if I can sniff out who the secret character is.

Finally tomorrow I get to start learning magic!

Chapter 3 Part 2: Of Magic and Men

I had gotten so distracted by the entrance ceremony and tripping over capture targets I had almost forgotten that I am here LEARNING MAGIC! The first class of the day was essentially general studies where they had crammed math, literature, and socio-politics all together. Maria and I had that class together so it was nice to start the day with her. The general studies class was fairly easy but interesting nonetheless. While the mathematic part was barely algebra, the literature and socio-political portions really interested me. This was an entirely foreign society to me. So it was fun to listen about what written works were considered required reading and how the political climate of the kingdom was currently. The professor, whose name I didn't catch, didn't dive into details today, but I'm interested to learn how a game world develops with non-game elements.

After general studies, Maria and I had to go our separate ways. While our classes are nearly identical, the academy operated more like a college and split the students up to take the same class at different times. Maria was pretty confused about the concept. She had only experienced a Japanese secondary school, so the class would stay the same and the teachers would rotate in. Having to walk to different classrooms to meet the teachers was strange to her.

The class I was heading to now was something called Magical Theory. If I had to guess, I doubt there is any spell casting in this class. Something with the name theory implies textbook learning.

I found the classroom easy enough. Maria had pointed out that I did in fact have a campus map, which I'm embarrassed to have forgotten about. Once I had the map in hand, I was able to navigate the campus with little problems.

The classroom had double-wide desks that sat two students per desk. I guess I am going to have a desk mate. Hopefully, it's someone I will be able to get along with. The room was almost full by the time I entered and I didn't want to disturb the friend groups that had already formed. I slide into a seat near the back of the classroom near the window. I always prefered window seats. If the lecture became boring, I would be able to look outside and hopefully entertain myself with some real or imaginary drama.

I found myself staring out the window while the class bell was ringing. I felt the presence of someone sit down next to me.

"Hello, my chickadee! We meet again," a familiar voice cooed into my ear.

Turning to the vocal offender, I don't bother to masked the disgusted look on my face. Duke Playboy was grinning his annoying shit-eating grin while his red hair flopped around in his face. Why can't I get away from these capture targets?

It takes all my effort to stay civil. This is for Maria. I only have to tolerate this until I know what route she will be taking. "Greetings, your grace," I once again emphasis his title hoping he gets the hint I want to keep a clear line between us.

"I'm very pleased to be able to enjoy this class with such fine scenery." Gross. I really can't stand this flirtatious borderline sexual harassment way of speaking he has.

"And I am looking forward to a peaceful class," I say extra nicely. But somehow I doubt the class with be anything peaceful.

"Duke Victor!" a girl calls out. "You should come sit next to me! I can share my macaroons with you." Yes please. Go share macaroons with that girl.

"Aw, my nightingale, if there were but enough of me to go around. But I have an unfulfilled date I'm quite impatient to schedule."

Suddenly I am the object of several death glares in the room. Are you kidding me? Dear Maria, this playboy jerk is making it hard for me not to commit murder. Would you be upset if we reduce your capture targets by one? But I am better than this jerk. I can outmanoeuvre him.

"Oh, my lady," I saw with my attention on the girl who had spoken. "Please don't let me get in the way of your macaroons. Feel free to trade seats with me!" I say as I'm quickly grabbing my things to move.

Luckily this girl was just as quick to jump to my offer so we swapped before Duke Playboy was able to react to what happened. While I was upset that I lost my precious window seat, it was well worth the trade. Now seated in the center of the classroom I can only sense him drilling holes into my head.

I hear the professor clear his throat to get the room's attention. He's a handsome sort of man with sandy brown hair pulled into a low side ponytail. He's wearing a pair of rimless glasses and a tasteful tweed jacket. He has that sort of hot nerd vibe to him.

"Welcome to your first day of Magical Theory. While I can't promise the subject isn't dry and boring, I will do my best to keep you all from falling asleep." There are a few laughs around the classroom at his speech. I had a feeling this wasn't going to be the most action-packed class. But I am still looking forward to it. "In addition to teaching the first years like you Magical Theory, I also instruct the 2nd year light magic students. I'm sure there are a few of you I'll have the pleasure of teaching again next year."

Wait. Light magic....

"My name is Professor Alan McGreggor," he finishes.

I let out a quiet noise of disgust. I take back all my thoughts about this guy being good looking.

And somewhere two desks behind me, someone notices my attitude shift.

Chapter 3 Part 3: Of Magic and Men

Maria and I had made plans to meet up for lunch. The dining hall was more considerably packed than when I had gone yesterday. Now that the students were locked into a schedule, that meant everyone was trying to eat around the same time. We had to sit at the end of a long community table shared by several students. So I knew our conversation regarding capture targets once again will have to wait until we were alone in our room together.

"How was magical theory?" Maria asks me after we place our orders.

"It was actually really interesting! And as much as I don't want to admit it, Professor McGreggor did a decent job keeping it entertaining."

"See. It was unfair of you to judge him so quickly."

"I still think he's a creepo pedophile! But as long as he doesn't make a move on you or any other student, then I will graciously acknowledge he might be a good teacher," I say as I wave my hand dismissively. Out of the corner of my eye, someone slides quietly into the seat next to me. I notice Maria get wide-eyed so I turn to see who it was.

"I'm supposed to eat with people," Lord Simon says quietly. Maria and I exchange smiles. Lord Simon might be a year older, but somehow I can't help to think of him as a kid brother.

"You are most welcome to join us any time, Lord Simon," I say to him. He nods slightly to me. Since I ready know getting him to join the conversation will be too much work, I continue with Maria.

"What class did you go to?"

"Combat basics."

"Oh! I have that last. Did you get sweaty?"

Maria chuckles. "A bit. I'm jealous you have yours late in the day. I'm worried when the class becomes more intense that I will be gross for the entire rest of the day!"

"They don't make girls work that hard," Lord Simon interjects. Sweet baby Jesus, did he just engage in conversation!

"Well, that's sexist!" I say to him. And he looks at me like I just kicked a puppy. "Not you! I didn't mean your sexist! Just the idea that the girls get to do less or work less. Don't some girls end up choosing combat magic?"

"Sometimes," he answers. "But it's pretty rare."

"That's because they aren't given the same chance as the boys to become proficient at it! If more girls were pushed to mastering the basics, then maybe more would find that they like it and chose combat magic!" I don't know why I'm defending this point so fiercely.

"I don't think I would want to specialize in combat magic," Maria says completely undermining my stance. I scowl at her. The annoying part is that Maria is destined to excel in anything she chooses. She has heroine plot armor.

"Well, maybe I will!"

"I can guess why," Maria says with a teasing tone and a look.

"That is not why!" I say much too loudly.

Actually it might be the truth, but my pride can't take hearing it out loud. I have a feeling that if I showed interest in any of the capture targets Maria would step aside to give me a chance. Which I absolutely don't want her to do. I'm the support character. I support her, not the other way around.

Luckily our food shows to stop the path of this particular conversation. Even though Lord Simon didn't order with us, he managed to have a meal delivered at the same time.

"You must have liked that chicken dish last time," I point out. He had ordered the same thing we ate yesterday.

"I already knew it was good. But you didn't get it again. Why?"

"I wanted to try this today," I shrug.

"Do you not like to eat the same things?"

"It's not like that. I do like to revisit meals. But I also like to explore new foods to see else I might like. Since we have only just started, I have a lot of menu items to try! Oy, Maria you got the salmon! Can I try it?"

"Mmm hmm," she says with her mouth full and spins the plate around to bring the salmon closer to me.

"Thanks!" I use my fork to grab a bite. "Mmmmmm! This is really good too. Do you want to try the roast I got."

Simon was staring intently at our interaction. "Do you want to try it too?" I ask him.

I can tell the question was making him think very hard. "You're ok if someone else eats your food?"

"Yeah. But only friends! I wouldn't like a stranger eating my food."

"Friends.....?"

"Yep! Go ahead!" I encourage him. He takes a tentative fork full of my roast and eats it gingerly. "Do you like it?"

"Yes," he answers softly.

"That's good! Now you know of two dishes you like on the menu!" He nods and shifts his focus back to his own plate.

Maria and I continue to catch each other up on what happened during our class separate from each other. I find out that Maria had combat basics with Prince Levi and by default, Sir Grey was also there. I tell her what I can about Duke Playboy being in my magical theory class, but it was hard to dive into specifics. I had to twist the story into being sad about losing my window seat in order to work him in.

"You have spell casting basics with me, right?" I ask Maria.

She nods. "We do! I made sure by checking our schedules but we were fated to have this class together." Fated? There must be an in-game reason. I make a mental note to ask why later.

"Good! I'd rather not have to give up my seat ---" I'm cut off by someone ramming into my elbow so hard I let out a yelp. As I look up, I see Lady Angelica making a big show of losing balance, complete with teacup. Ah shit, that's going to spill on Maria! I move to try to block it from spilling on her when the teacup suddenly stops mid-air. Maria and I are staring at it wide-eyed.

"Ah! L-lord Simon!" Maria exclaims. Lord Simon was using magic to prevent the teacup from spilling on Maria. Good job, Simon! Bonus points towards your capture route! And thank you stupid villainess for creating an opportunity for the capture target to save the heroine.

"Oh Lady Maria, Lady Christine. Forgive me, I didn't see you sitting there," she says condescendingly. "And Lord Simon," she quickly slides over to him. "Thank you so much for saving me from my blunder." She lightly pets his arm in an obvious attempt at flirting. I roll my eyes. Sadly, since Maria isn't on any specific route, we get to watch Angelica attempt to steal every capture target in the meantime.

Lord Simon started to look very uncomfortable from Angelica leaning so close to him. Poor thing. He doesn't seem like the sort who is experienced with women flirting with him. I grab the floating teacup so that he can release his spell. As I happen to look down into the cup I notice something strange. I don't think this is tea. It was jet black and had a thicker viscosity to it. Ink? This was very deliberate. Not wishing to stay any longer, I grab Maria by the arm and pull her up.

"Thank you, Lord Simon," I say with a slight bow, "for both your company today and you graciously saving Maria's uniform from ruin. Unfortunately, it seems the lunch hour is nearly at an end and since Maria and I are new, we should use this extra time to navigate to our next class. Peaceful blessings to you." I start to pull Maria away.

"Uh...." she stammers. "Peaceful blessings to both of you." I quickly walk her out of the dining hall. Thanks to Lord Simon, Maria got out of this round of bullying unscathed. But that means Angelica will double down her efforts next time. Best to leave when ahead!

Chapter 3 Part 4: Of Magic and Men

Maria and I got to the classroom well before anyone else so it gave us the privacy to truly catch up. Laying claim to my window seat, Maria sits next to me. This classroom has long tables set with groups of three. So the seat beside Maria remains free.

"So," I begin. "Combat Basics with Prince Levi AND Sir Grey?" I wiggle my eyebrows to entice her to share some juicy gossip.

"Nothing happened! Prince Levi IS in my class. But the girls and boys are separated, so we didn't really interact that much."

"For now. I played both of their routes and I very much remember a couple of events happening during that class. Though, I'm a little hazy on the details." I remember it had something to do with Lady Angelica both times though.

"It's fairly minor since the major flag events don't happen until the 2nd year. But with Sir Grey, there's an event where Angelica bullies the heroine during training. She ends up pushing her into a weapon's rack which starts to fall. Sir Grey reacts quickly and shields the heroine from getting hurt by the falling weapons."

"Right! There's a CG of him holding the heroine tightly!"

"It's a shame you aren't in the same class as me," Maria says giggling slightly. I just give her the stink eye. I have a feeling I will never escape the teasing about Sir Grey.

"What about Prince Levi?"

"It's when we are taught to channel our magic into the weapons. Since the heroine has water magic pretty early on, they partner them together assuming there would be less of a chance either of them hurting each other due to the magical affinities."

I nod along as Maria explains. The CG for that scene didn't include any sudden unintentional hugging but was of the Prince looking very handsome while wielding a fire sword.

"Hmmmmm. Sadly, this doesn't give us any idea of how long it will be before either of those events happen. But," I say with a slight pause, "it seems like the Prince's event could be missed if it doesn't trigger on the day you are told to channel your magic.....right?"

Maria stares in thought. "Maybe..... There are stat requirements to trigger the event. But this is real life. The professor is going to teach it to us no matter what and, likely, with a plan already set in the teaching curriculum."

"So we have to figure out how to get Prince Levi's event --" I cut myself off as I see a couple of students enter the classroom. The rest of this conversation will have to wait. We switch to talking about the school in general and the insignificant details of the class we shared apart. As the room starts to fill up, it becomes harder to talk without yelling at each other. I forgot what it was like in high school. I keep thinking of this school as a college, but in fact the students are still highschool aged. And when are high school students the loudest and most rowdy? After lunch. Everyone feels charged from eating and high on socializing with friends.

Just when I thought the room couldn't get louder, the female students start screaming. Not fear screaming, but fangirl screaming. Which Jonas brother has just walked in? I turn to look at the door. Obviously not a Jonas brother, but instead the Prince. Figures. I rub my temples.

"I SINCERELY HOPE WE DON'T HAVE TO LISTEN TO THIS EVERY FUCKING TIME WE COME TO THIS CLASS," I say yelling at Maria as a necessity. Maria shrugs at me. She seems unfazed by the fangirl screams.

Prince Levi walks towards our table and bows slightly. "Is this seat taken, ladies?" he asks with his perfect manners.

"N-no," Maria stammers. I simply affirm with nodding. Prince Levi sits down next to Maria and for the 2nd time today, I am assaulted by death stares. The room starts to quiet down as the bell for class starts sounding.

"And don't worry," he says smiling gently at both of us. "Eventually their voices will run dry, so you'll only have to endure it for a week or so." I laugh back with one of those scared embarrassed laughs.

I shrink in my chair. He fucking heard me.

The professor starts class and I only half pay attention to what she is saying. I keep side eyeing Maria and the Prince to gauge their relationship. Maria is completely focused on the class, so she's not giving me any hints. I dare not try to look too much at Prince Levi, because no matter how I spin it, it will only seem like I am another love struck dumb girl.

After the class ends, Prince Levi starts making small talk with Maria. Yes, yes very good. As much as I want to eavesdrop, I decide my departure would best suit the mood.

"I'll catch up with you later," I whisper to Maria as I quickly excuse myself. I don't bother to greet the Prince as I leave. It's best not to draw any more attention to myself.

I only have one class left for the day and I'm slightly worried that it might be this world's version of PE.

I walk briskly to the combat side of the academy. As I pass the groups of students that are loitering outside, I wonder how it is that even though I am a side character, I seem to be constantly bumping into the capture targets. Literally everywhere I go, I have run into one of them. Is this something that happened to the original Christine Eldergast? There's no way to know. Her time spent away from Maria was never discussed. Now I'm wishing that the game had one throw away line where she said, "Why do I keep bumping into these guys?" so I can relax knowing our meetings are by design. I need mob character friends. That's what I need to focus on tomorrow. I need to find friends to help me blend into the background.

When I get to the combat building, I see a grizzled looking man standing by the main entrance. I think I know him. He's the combat instructor. A former solider of the kingdom.......I can't remember much else. I walk tentatively towards him.

"You!" he shouts at me. "First year!"

"Yes?!" I screech.

"You here for combat basics?"

"Yes, sir!"

"Good. Inside turn to the right at the hall. That's the women's changing salon. Don't go left. I don't feel like hearing your screaming," he says with authority.

"Yes, sir. Of course, sir," I say as I scurry in. Why am I answering him like a fresh recruit? Maybe it can't be helped when in the presence of someone you know killed some guys.

Go right. Go right. Go right. I chant to myself.

Chapter 4 Part 1: Grinding Stats

I ache.

Combat basics is kicking my ass. Sir Sizemore did not hold back. The whole class spends one week on each weapon type to determine what each of us should specialize in. We were randomly assigned weapons. I had the worst sort of luck starting with a greatsword my first week then a mace in my second. I envy the students with daggers. Light. Fast. Did I mention light? The first two weeks flew by without incident. Maria and I had settled into a rhythm. We both joked it was monotonous because it's a game world. If this was the game, I would be working on grinding stats. But since this is real life - well weird real life - I haven't had the inclination to grind any stats, especially when I know I'm not the heroine. Classes are starting to get interesting even if we haven't actually used any magic yet. Maria has though. Since she was identified as a water user so early on, she was able to start her affinity tutoring right away and, get this, Lord Simon is her mentor! He still joins us for lunch and says very little, but Maria told me when he gets excited about magic he talks a lot. I'm sad I haven't been able to see it. I've tried a couple of times at lunch asking him magic-related questions to get him to talk, but I never have any success.

"Want to go to town?!" Maria suddenly asks.

I look up from my studies to see her peering at me from her bed. Last weekend we didn't go anywhere. We were both so overwhelmed from starting the academy we had just explored the school grounds instead. It was good for us. Since it was the first weekend, almost all the students had flocked to the nearby town and left the campus fairly empty.

"I guess," I say indifferently. "Was there somewhere, in particular, you wanted to go?"

"Well," she says as she sits up from her lounging position, "do you remember the shops from the game?"

"Kinda.....There was the place that sold the gifts.....?"

"Yep! Frederick's. That's where you could purchase gifts for the capture targets."

I nod along. "And a dress shop......"

"There were two. Rose Boutique for casual wear that was cheaper and The Silver Nightengale for the really fancy dresses like ballgown."

"Right."

"I really want to see the shops in person!" Maria was starting to get excited. It happened easily when she starts talking about game details.

"Well then, we should call the maids to help us get ready."

"Yay!" Maria squeals. She jumps from her bed to ring the bell to summon Lindsay and Julie. Responding quickly, they help us change into more appropriate clothes to wear around town. Having worn the simple and very practical school uniform for two weeks, I wasn't thrilled about stuffing myself into a fluffy princess dress again. I chose my most simple dress, a warm yellow that complimented my violet eyes. It still wasn't my true taste, but it had the least amount of ribbons and bows decorating it. To be honest, I wish I could rip all the extra decorations off. I am jeans and t-shirt kind of girl. I look at Maria who chose a pale blue dress that had significantly more bows than mine. I wonder if I can get away with wearing pants. I know Maria wouldn't think twice about it, but how much of an uproar would it cause here in gameland?

"We can use the teleportation circle to get to town!" Maria says slightly hopping from excitement. Ok. That does sound exciting. I've never teleported anywhere.

"Did you learn how to use teleportation magic already?" I ask her as we make our way out of the dorm.

"Oh no! We probably won't learn that until much later this year. Lord Simon gave me teleportation scrolls!" She thrusts a piece of paper into my hand. It's rectangular in shape and has red writing in strange symbols on it.

"Maria....these seem.... familiar?" I ask hesitantly.

"Oh yeah! They look exactly like bujeok!"

"Bujeok?"

"Ah, how do I explain....." she ponders for a moment. "In Korea they have shamans. And they make talismans you can buy. Those are bujeok."

"Oh right! I never knew their name. I would see them in the Korean dramas! Usually, the mom or someone would buy them for their daughter having bad luck or something."

"Right," Maria says with a giggle. "Or to protect from ghosts! One of my favorite dramas was about a ghost who was trying to find a man to seduce."

"Oh, I saw that one! And she ends up possessing the girl who was in love with her boss!"

We reminisce about the drama while we walk to the teleportation circle. It is located in the inner courtyard of the spell caster building.

"Ah, Lady Maria, Lady Christine good to see you two out and about." We turn to see who addressed us.

"Hello Professor McGreggor," Maria says. I inhale sharply instead. It doesn't escape Maria's notice and she squeezes my arm. Fine. I'll be nice.

"Greetings to you, Professor," turning my customer service mode on. "Forgive our rudeness, we were hoping to use the teleportation circle to head into town."

"Yes, yes, of course. I didn't mean to intrude. Are you.....able.....to use the teleportation circle?" he asked while eyeing Maria. Tsk, this creep.

"We have scrolls!" I say waving mine around to grab his attention.

"Ah, how resourceful. Please don't let me keep you then."

"Thank you, Professor," Maria says. "Would you --" I grab her hand and yank her.

"Peaceful greetings to you Professor!" I call out as I pull Maria away.

"Christine......" she says quietly with a tone I know to be disapproving.

"Don't talk to him."

Chapter 4 Part 2: Grinding Stats

AHHHHHHHHHHHHHHHHHHHhhhhhhhhhhhhhhhh!

The world swirled around me in bright blue. Am I screaming? I think I'm screaming.

"Christine?" Maria tugs on me and I barely hear her. What. Dafaq. Was. That?!

We are standing in the town center on the teleporter platform. In every movie, book, manga, comic, anime, game...... you name it.... teleporting was no big deal. You have some amazing visual, sprinkle in some magic or technobabble, and viola, you are whisked away to somewhere quickly and easily. But no. NO! It was horrible! It was the first drop of a rollercoaster, the moments before realizing you're going to hit the car in front of you, watching a glass cup fall, holding your breath too long, and the tingle of your leg falling asleep all crammed into one sensation.

"Christine," I hear Maria this time as I stare at her wide-eyed. She gently pulls me off the platform. I wobble violently as I'm being ushered along.

"Here, I'll take her," I hear a man's voice say.

"Oh, thank you," Maria responds to his help.

I feel a strong arm wrap around my waist as my weight is being lifted slightly to allow me to stumble to a nearby bench. As I fall into the seat, I collapse my head into my hands. The world is spinning.

"Does she suffer from telesickness?" I hear the man ask.

"I don't know," Maria says with a shake in her voice. "It's the first time we have teleported."

"Was this her first time ever teleporting?" I hear he emphasizes the word ever indicating he sounds shocked I would have never teleported before.

"Uh......." Maria hesitates. "Maybe?"

"Tsk," I hear him click his tongue. "I guess so. I doubt she would have stepped foot in the teleporter had she known. Wait here. I'll grab a sickness potion from the apothecary."

"Thank you," I hear the footsteps walk away. "Christine...." Maria coos like she is comforting a child. I feel her rub my back. "Hang tight. The medicine will be here soon."

"Uh hmm," I groan out an answer without looking up. My head is still spinning and I feel a pit at the bottom of my stomach that I am barely keeping control of. I focus on the sounds of the town in an attempt to stabilize myself.

I barely noticed my surroundings when we arrived, but I know we are in an outdoor plaza, and from the sounds of things, it's pretty lively. I can hear the chatter of the crowd, close enough to be loud, but far enough away to be indistinct. I also hear the racket of carriages and horses moving up and down what I assume to be a road close by. That makes sense considering this would be this world's version of a mass transit hub, like an airport or subway depot.

After what feels like an eternity, I hear footsteps approach.

"I have the sickness potion. Lady Christine, can you sit up? You will feel much better if you can drink this," the man says.

I groan and force myself upright. I reach blindly and I feel the vial put into my hands. Without thought, I quickly drink the contents. Yuck. It tastes like someone liquified Vicks and mixed it with lavender dish soap to create this unholy concoction. But despite the horrid taste, both my vertigo and stomach start to settle. Not wishing to rush things, I drop my head back into my hands waiting for full relief.

"Thank you so much, your grace," Maria says. "How much was the potion?"

"Not worth mentioning," he says politely.

"But I wish to repay your kindness." Despite reading my fair share of romance stories in every media available, hearing this type of conversation in real life gives me a different type of nausea. Huh? I guess despite wishing for romance it turns out I actually can't stand cliche romance. Seriously. If a man appeared in front of me with a Big Mac and a Coke, I would marry him on the spot.

"If you want to repay me, all I request is for your lovely company. Pending, of course, your friend's health."

Does this guy think he's being slick? I better brave sitting up. I have to beat this guy back before Maria agrees to something random. She already has five capture targets to juggle.

"That's not something we can accommodate sadly," I say weakly as I look up. The potion had helped considerably. I blink a few times to get my surroundings into focus and look at the gentleman kneeling in front of me. His red hair was blowing gently in the wind as he gave me a wide smile.

"Glad to see you back to your senses, my chickadee."

"Ugh, great. Saved by Duke Playboy."

"Christine!" Maria says shocked and I look at her as she is staring at me in horror. Oh shit. I said that out loud didn't I? I turn my attention back to Duke.... what is his name?

He laughs. "Duke Playboy?" he says during his laughing fit.

I roll my eyes. Well, at least I don't have to worry about him being offended. What a flippant man.

"I'm so sorry! Please forgive my friend! She must be shocked and, uh, isn't feeling well right now," Maria is stammering trying to cover my blunder.

"Oh, no no, it's quite alright!" he says still laughing. "But, you most certainly owe me now!" He says looking directly at me. Can I kick him?

"I will be certain to pay you back for the cost of the potion," I say as politely as I can.

"Oh no, that won't do at all! You also owe for services rendered! I ran with such urgency that the King himself would have praised my speed," he says with an air of arrogance.

"Right," I deadpan. "I'll add an appropriate delivery fee."

"Excellent!" he says grabbing my arm and dragging me to my feet. "There's a wonderful cafe nearby. I'm sure you wanting to wash away the lingering taste of that dreadful potion."

How annoying. Yes.

"It is dreadful, but I can manage."

"This way!" he ignores my attempt to deny the gathering.

Duke Formally Known as Playboy, grabs my hand and offers his left arm to Maria to escort. Before I can protest, Maria takes his arm and he pulls me forward.

I officially hate teleporting.

Chapter 4 Part 3: Grinding Stats

Today's excursion was so far the most miserable thing I've done since my reincarnation. Aside from the horrid experience of teleportation, I am now stuck in a tea cafe - boring - with Duke Playboy - whose name is Duke Victor Mossgrave as Maria slyly reminded me - and I am forced to listen to his obnoxious flirting. He really was indiscriminate with the flirting. He flirted with the waitress. He flirted with every lady who walked by or glanced his way with his stupid grin and leering gaze. If Maria hadn't told me about his backstory and ultimate story arch and the fact that apparently, he will settle down if he falls in love with her, I would have just bought another one of those nasty potions and risked a return teleport back to the academy.

As I was staring at my cup ginger tea, which helped calm my stomach but did nothing reduce the after taste of the potion I drank, I felt someone kicking me under the table. I looked up at Maria who was looking at me with bug eyes. I scowled at Duke Victor. Did he do or say something that crossed the line? Instead, he irritatingly smiled at me. Maria cleared her throat.

"Christine," she said quietly. "CG event."

"Huh?"

"CG event," she said through gritted teeth while nodding towards Duke Victor.

"Now?!" I finally caught on. Apparently this moment was supposed to be significant. She beckoned me to lean closer to whisper in my ear.

"Yes, but you're not supposed to be here. I saw Lady Angelica enter downstairs. She's going to come up here and see me with the Duke and he's going to save me from her bullying."

"Oh. So I need to bugger off?" I whispered back.

"Now ladies, I am quite jealous I don't get to hear the tantalizing gossip that must be forming right now," Duke Victor cooed at us. He's so annoying! I have to think of a way to excuse myself and fast.

"Forgive me, your grace," I said trying to remind him to act appropriately. "I have little stomach for desserts right now. I'm going to catch a carriage back to the academy." I stood and curtsied a bit to take my leave.

"I'd be happy to accompany you. I couldn't possibly have you fall prey to illness again!" he said with a hint of mockery in his tone.

"No!" I cringed as I realized I said that a little too strongly. "No, please stay with Maria and keep her company. We had been cooped up all week and I feel guilty if I had to drag her back with me." I heard laughter coming up the stairs. A very peculiar type of laughter. A villainesses laughter. Shit! Time to get a move on. "Thank you for your hospitality! Goodbye!" And I bolted out of there. Since there was only one staircase leading to the upstairs, I circled around the room the long way allowing Lady Angelica to get to the top and head toward the direction of Maria. I waited as her entourage of ladies appeared and I snuck onto the staircase behind them.

"Oh! Duke Mossgrave! I didn't know you were here! How fortuitous!" I heard her trill. I spared once parting glance at Maria and silently wished her luck before descending the stairs quickly. I exited the cafe as quickly as I could. When I got to the busy street, I realized that I had no idea where I was. I was so ill when I was brought here I barely paid attention to where we went. But as I saw the cobblestone street and the variety of shops I only felt excitement. Well, I might as well go shipping! I did bring money to spend and I might as well reward myself for the miserable day thus far.

Picking no particular direction I started walking. Little did I know, but a certain redhead had noticed I was not walking in the direction towards the public carriages.

As I walked the street I admired the window displays. Back home, malls and storefronts would have window displays, but I never paid much attention to them. Lifeless mannequins with whatever trend clothing were always on display with some lame company slogan to go with the season. Christmas time was always the worst. They had to incorporate some stupid non-denomination holiday pun. "Jingle your bells this Holiday Season." Or something equally stupid. But these window displays were amazing! This was loosely a version of Victorian England. There wasn't TV commercials or billboards advertising your store. The only way to gain customers was word of mouth and with the flashy storefront to get them inside!

The storefronts spared no expense! Beautifully decorated signs denoted the name of the store, while the windows were elegantly arranged to feature whatever flashy product they could sell to gain attention. The hattery, which I definitely won't step foot in, had the biggest, grandest, ugliest hats on display with all sorts of accessories hanging mercilessly from them. Of course, it was one of the larger stores and had a stream of women going in and out creating no rest for the doorbell.

Moving further down the street I heard a small boy call out. "Combat Wizards Tourny! Prizes for the winners! Combat Wizards Tourny!" I walked quickly up to the boy.

"Can anyone enter?" I asked. Generally speaking, the game was more popular among boys.

"Yes, my lady! Only 10 silver to enter! It's about to start soon too!"

"Great! Where do I sign up?"

"Over there," he pointed at the entrance of a small garden. "The sign-up booth is in the middle of Parnas Park."

"Thank you!" I said gleefully as I made my way to the park.

Chapter 4 Part 4: Grinding Stats

The sun shone brightly as I readied my spells. I smiled viciously at my enemy, who both sweating profusely and cursing very colorfully under his breath. I had mercilessly clawed my way to the final battle of the Combat Wizards Tourny. The best part was there wasn't a capture target in sight! If I had to use game terms, this tourny was filled with a bunch of nameless NPCs that served as leveling fodder. The first few battles were so easy I sincerely worried about the intelligence level of the players. The opponents had gotten progressively better, but it wasn't until the last couple that the skill level wasn't offensive.

My current opponent was in the exact same situation that I was on my first game with Sir Grey. Despite knowing that this was the final game, he had taken one look at me, a young noblewoman, and underestimated my ability. While I hadn't exactly underestimated Sir Grey, I was too star stuck to think straight at first. His turn ends and all eyes fall to me. While I really wanted to produce my best villainess cackle, I suppress my desire and calmly play my hand cleanly killing his last wizard and ending the game. The gathered crowd claps politely but I can tell no one was very excited I had won. Oh well, not that I care.

"Congratulations, miss!" the elderly game master tenderly grasp my hand. He was one of those grandfatherly types, so I couldn't help but smile at him. "It's not often such a young lady shows such talent!" He placed my hand into the crock of his arm to lead me back to the table where everyone had signed up at.

When we arrive at the table a middle-aged man servant greets us.

"Here is your reward, my lady," he says while handing me a sword. My confusion was apparent on my face so the game master felt obligated to explain. "This short sword was crafted by Dragon Scale Armory. I assure you it is of the highest quality."

"Oh - forgive me. I mean no disrespect to the quality of the sword. To be honest, I hadn't considered the rewards at all. I simply entered to have fun."

The old game master chuckled softly. "All the better for it! Here -" he hands me the sword, "keep it for yourself or gift it to a young man!" He says with a wink.

"Thank you very much," I say with a curtsy.

The tourny had taken a couple of hours so the sun was starting to set. The park was clearing out quickly as everyone hurried off to their evening excursions. Not sure what to do now, I take my new sword and head to the park exit.

"Lady Christine!" I hear someone call my name. As I look around to see who had called for me, I see a decidedly attractive man walking with long strides towards me. Ah, yes. My favorite capture target.

"Sir Grey! What a surprise. What brings you here?"

"I wanted to ask the same, but I couldn't help but to watch your final game, so my curiosity was quickly sated."

"Ah, ha...." I nervously shift suddenly aware of the sword I'm awkwardly holding. There's a small glint in his eye as he notices.

"A Dragon Scale Armory sword?" he asks.

"Yes, so I've been told."

"They make quality weapons. Do you intend on keeping it?"

"Honestly I don't know. I hadn't given any thought to it. I haven't made it to short swords in combat basics. I got stuck with a great sword my first week and mace this week. My arms have turned to jelly!"

Laughing slightly, Sir Grey offers me his arm indicating he intended to escort me out of the park. "That is an unlucky draw for your first two weeks. But, you should consider keeping it for now. At least until you have a chance to see if you have any skill or interest in short swords."

"Your advice is extremely reasonable," I nod along. Out of all the capture targets he really is the easiest to talk to.

"Have you given any thought to your specialization?"

"Not at all. I haven't had a chance to check my affinity yet."

"Well, affinity aside, you do have the choice of spell casting or combat focus."

"True. But greatswords and maces haven't exactly sold me on the idea."

"Haha. I suppose not," he said warmly. "But if you do decide to keep the sword, don't forget to have it enchanted once you know your affinity."

"How so?" Weapon enchants? This was not something the game mentioned. Well at least, the two routes that I did play it was never mentioned. This sounded like something set squarely in RPG territory rather than an innocuous dating sim.

"Well, the sword on its own is very fine. But you will want to channel your magical element through it. So that's where enchanting comes in. Ah, sorry. I completely forgot they don't cover this until much later in the first year."

"No need to apologize! Once you mentioned it, I rather inferred what it would pertain to. Are there multiple enchants to choose from? Or once my affinity is set, is there just one type?" In most RPGs, weapon enchants can run the gauntlet of types depending on build. I hadn't considered that Otome World might have other genres mixed in.

Sir Grey cocked an eyebrow at me as we walked. "A very astute question from someone who only just heard about weapon enchanting."

"Ah, heh. Sorry."

"It wasn't my intention to disparage you. I am just pleasantly surprised your first thought would be to inquire about enchantment types. And before I digress too far, yes there are a variety of types to choose from. Some of which are exceeding hard to obtain as it can take the expertise of someone exceptionally skilled."

"Ah and likely not cheaply either!"

"Keenly observed." We suddenly stopped as a storefront took Sir Grey's attention. I turned to look to see what had grabbed him. The storefront had a variety of plush toys and colorful ribbons hanging in the display. If I had to guess, it was a toy or children's store. Ah, the sister! We had been talking about such adult topics I had completely forgotten this guy was a major sis-con. The wheels in my head were turning. I know he wants to go in and shop for his sister. But that's only because I have game knowledge. In real life, he hasn't told me about her. So how do I navigate this? I don't have a younger sibling at home to use as an excuse. Oh, that would have been too easy! Can I pretend to want to go in? Would that be weird?

I glance up at his face and I can see the gears grinding. Ah, forget my pride. He wants to go in so bad I can tell he likely won't think twice about me. Well, time to pretend to be the type of girl I really loath.

"Heeeeeeeeeeeeeh??!" I exclaim really loudly which startles Sir Grey. "That's so cuuuuuuuuuuuuute!"

"Huh?" he says looking confused.

"That!" I point at a random plush of a rabbit in the window. "It's too cute! I want to go see it! Do you mind? I'll be super fast! You can wait out here if you don't want to go in!" I lay it on thick. It's saccharine and disgusting. Goodbye, my pride. It's been nice knowing you.

"Oh. Oh! No! We can go in! I don't mind at all!" I glace at his excited face. He can barely contain himself now. Well, it looks like I wasn't the only one who just left their pride on the sidewalk.

"Yay!" Uh, gag me. "Let's go!" And I very unlady-like drag him into the store.

We are greeted with an explosion of pink decore that makes my eyes water slightly. This store has exactly one target demographic: rich, spoiled, young girls who dream of being a princess and only have pink as a favorite color.

"How perfect!" Sir Grey says quietly. Ok. This store has exactly two target demographics: rich, spoiled, young girls who dream of being a princess, and only have pink as a favorite color and their sis-con brothers.

Sir Grey almost immediately forgets I exist and heads directly to the wall of plushes. I watch as he starts inspecting each one. I have to admit, watching him check for softness was pretty damn adorable.

"Can I help you find anything?" a matronly woman in a pink and white striped dress walks over to me. In this situation one would assume I am the one shopping, so obviously she chose to obtain the attention of the person with the purchasing decisions.

"Actually I'm good. But," I lean over to whisper to her, "my friend here looked like he really wanted to see the plushes and I didn't want to embarrass him. So I pretended to want to come inside. Can you help me do some reconnaissance?" The store employee chuckles slightly.

"I understand. I've seen this before. It means there is a child at home that they wish to dote on," she says quietly back to me. The woman slides up next to Sir Grey. "Good day young man. If you are looking for a birthday gift, I recommend the fuzzy pony. It's one of our most popular. Young girls tend to have a phase in which they wish to ride horses but are too little to do so." Oh. She's good! In one sentence, she has opened the door for him to correct her about the relationship of the gift receiver and to ascertain the age of the child.

"Oh! Well, big no on ponies. She had that phase last year. But oddly enough, she has an odd fascination with pigs."

"Pigs?" the lady chuckled that warm mom laugh. "How old is the young miss?"

"Five!" he says practically beaming.

"We have just the thing!" She walks a little further into the store and Sir Grey follows her. If he was a dog, his tail would be wagging a mile a minute. "How about this one?" He takes the pig plush, which I have to say was pretty cute, from her, and gives it a squeeze. He then emulates hugging it to test its fluffiness. Dear Lord, I am about to die. If this was a manga, the nosebleed would be gushing right now.

"Perfect! I'll take it!" And without a second glance, he goes to the counter to pay. I wait patiently as the transaction unfolds. The woman gives me a quick wink and hands the plush to Sir Grey in a bright pink shopping bag. "Thank you for your expert assistance," he bows slightly ever the gentleman. As he turns to head out the door he sees me waiting and the realization that I once again exist slowly crosses his face. "Lady C-christine...." he stammers, the panic setting in.

I smile back at him. "I'm glad we had a chance to stop," I said as I held out my hand indicating I expected him to continue our walk. Sir Grey clears his throat nervously and quickly walks over to me to offer his arm.

As we leave the store I glance up and notice his very red ears. Oh, poor thing. You found your trampled pride waiting for you at the curb. I wasn't sure what to say to make the mood less awkward so I chose to wait for him to say something. We walked silently for a little while when I noticed a few side-eye glances from strangers. Do we look weird? I glance at Sir Grey, then down at myself.

Realization dawns on me and I can't hold in my laughter.

"What - is so funny?" he asks tentatively.

"What a pair we make!" I stammer out during my fit. "You, an immaculately dressed knight, are holding the frilliest pink bag I have ever seen and me-" laughter interrupts my speech. "I'm holding a damn sword!"

Sir Grey stopes to assess the situation and after a moment his laughter joins mine. "It is indeed ridiculous!"

Update from the Author

To everyone who has made it this far, thanks for reading! I hope you are enjoying the story.

Updates are going to delayed for the next few weeks as I am in the process of moving. I've also decided that it would likely be more enjoyable for the reader to release chapters in full rather by parts as I have been doing. I'm a novice writer doing this as a quarantine past time, so I think it would do me good as well since I can edit the chapter to be a bit more cohesive.

In the meantime, I would love to hear everyone's thoughts so far! The story is being written organically, so while I know the general big picture, it will be fun for me to find out how everyone feels about the capture targets!

See ya soon!

--Lady Conure

Chapter 5 Part 1: A Contest of Wits

✶ ****Thanks for hanging tight, everyone! I had a big move and finally have the time to get back into this.*****

It turns out both Maria and I had lucrative trips to town. She spent entirely too much time trying to apologize for my teleportation sickness, which was just silly. It's not like it was her fault. Since the sword was a bit inconspicuous, I had to tell my story first. We had a good laugh at the expense of Sir Grey. Maria got her CG event. Lady Veronica tried the whole tea spilling thing again! Couldn't this bully try a different tactic? After Duke Victor - as much as it pains me, I need to stop calling him mean nicknames - smoothed things over, he took Maria to The Silver Nightengale to buy a new dress. Of course, he had to do that thing they do in all the rich guy takes poor girl shopping dramas - fashion show! I'm actually glad I skipped that. I've never been one to try on a ton of clothes and parade them around friends. Those scenes in the dramas always look like an endurance test. Maria was quite happy with her new light blue dress and her opinion of Duke Victor was much higher than mine.

The following week at school didn't differ much from the previous weeks. Although I found out that I was changing to a short sword soon, so I am pretty excited about that. I'll get an idea if I want to keep the sword I bought. Since I finished my classes before Maria, I was wandering around the common grounds when I noticed a crowd gathering around one of the notice boards. I make my way over to see what the fuss is all about, although I can't get very close. As I am hoping slightly to see over everyone's head I feel someone tap on my shoulder.

"It's rather unbecoming to be hopping up and down like a frog."

Lady Veronica. Great.

Since I avoided her last weekend, she so far hasn't thought of me as a threat. I'm not super thrilled to be socializing with her, she is someone I can gather intelligence from. That is until she goes bat shit crazy when the love conquest picks up with Maria.

"Oh, Lady Veronica," I coo and curtsy. "I apologize for my unsightly behavior, but I can't fathom what the excitement is all about."

"It's just the announcement for The Hankerchief Contest," she says with a shrug of her hand.

"Hankerchief contest? I assume you design a handkerchief and someone important like the prince judges it?" If that's the case, Maria has already won.

"What a simple mind you have," she says with disgust. "It's much more than just a normal contest. All the eligible noblemen choose a color handkerchief and is assigned a random number. The eligible ladies then pick one and design it. Then there's a hunt where we find who the handkerchief belongs to."

"Oh. So you have no idea if the handkerchief your working on belongs to the prince or not." Let's be honest. Maria has main character aura. She's going to get the guy she likes the best no matter what.

"Yes, yes. So your color choice is extremely important. For instance, the Royal Family is likely to choose dark blue."

"But don't pick black!" one of Veronica's lackys shouts out suddenly. All the girls start gossiping about how horrible that would be.

"Why?"

"Because," the lacky explains, "it belongs to The Demon of the North! He is the only one who ever submits a black handkerchief."

"Demon of the North?"

"I seriously question the education you recieved at home, Lady Christine!" Veronica exclaims. Tsk. I'm putting up with this because I am (mentally) a mature adult and recongnize when I need to intelligence gather.

"It wasn't for my parent's lack of trying. I got sick shortly before coming to the academy and suffer from amnesia. Sadly, I have forgotten a lot." I pout a little bit to really sell the sad tale.

"I knew something was wrong with your brain." A sigh escapes Veronica's lips. "The Demon of the North is Archduke Ellis Wintergard. He's the commander of The Black Guard, cousin to Prince Levi - on his mother's side, and holds the vast lands of the Wintergard estate in the north. He's a brutal warrior and someone to stay away from."

"And he participates in The Handkerchief Contest? He's not married?"

"He's 28 and not married. Honestly, I pitty the poor lady that ends up with his hand. What a miserable life she would have."

Wow. This guy is rich, had a superior title, in line for the crown (sorta), young and none of these girls want to take a stab at him. Is he a villian? I don't remeber him in the game at all. Although I didn't play all the routes, so maybe Maria knows more.

"Ah......" I say like I totally understand. "Thank you for your insightful warnings." A thought suddenly occures to me. Lady Veronica is destined to go after whichever capture target Maria chooses. Maria hasn't really made any strong advances towards anyone in particular but maybe Maria and Veronica are connected by fate. If Veronica has strong feelings towards someone specific, perhaps Maria does too and is too dense to realise it yet. It wouldn't suprise me if she doesn't understand her own feelings. "Is there anyone in particular you are hoping to catch?"

She narrows her eyes at me. "Why should I tell you?"

"Oh come now!" I fake joviality. "While it's true we are all looking to match a good match, I am not such a poor sport to intentionally steal a man away from another lady. I only desire to know your preference so that I may strike the man from my list. I would be at an exteme disadvatage if I went against you and honestly, no man is worth such a fight."

"Hmmmm..... I suppose there is some sense in you," she says with a sigh. "Obviously I will be aiming for either of the Princes, though I would say since Prince Levi is the crown prince, he is top choice."

The manner in which she delivered this was done in such a way I could tell she was saying what we all expected her to say. I guess she won't fully commit to someone until Maria does.

"I can't wait to see both princes!" a lacky squeals with joy.

Ah right. The older brother who for some reason is not the crown prince and is rumored to be one of the capture targets of Doki Doki Love Academy 2.

"Will the 1st prince come?" I ask. "I thought he had disapeared somewhere."

"He hasn't disappeared!" Veronica hisses. "He's been in Rubar securing peace for both kingdoms."

"How noble!" another lacky sighs like a love struck puppy.

"So......he's been in peace talks with Rubar this whole time? But will make time for The Handkerchief Contest?"

"Like he would miss an event with single ladies," Veronica almost growls. Interesting. It seems as though she has no interest in the 1st prince. Is it because of his reputation? Or that he isn't the crown prince? Or because this is a game world and she is only capible of wanting capture targets? "Anyways, we have lingered long enough. Lady Christine, while I have - enjoyed - our conversation I almost forgot to chastise you on something important."

"Chastise? Me.....?"

"Yes! You went to town without a hat! Such a shameless show of impropriety!"

"Ah...haha... well.... I did have a hat on, you see," (a lie) "but I became sick after using the teleporter and in my stupior I lost it somewhere. And I was too ill to think on it."

...

She is doing that thing that only villianesses can do. Staring down her nose with disgust.

"Don't let it happen again. Ladies!" and with an air she turns walking away with lackies in tow.

Chapter 5 part 2: A Contest of Wits

Maria didn't have a chance to even sit down before I started pumping her for information about this handkerchief contest.

"Handkerchief contest?" Maria asks perplexed. "I don't know anything about it."

"Really? Isn't this an event in the game?"

"No. There wasn't anything like this."

"I wonder why? This type of event seems like something that would happen."

"I agree with you. A contest that pits the villainess and the heroine against each other for attention from the capture targets is exactly something that should be in the game. Also, this would be a good spot for CGs."

Realizing I've been leaning forward causing my back to be stiff, I sit back to relax to enjoy my tea, and think. So we have an event that has all the callings of an otome event yet isn't actually in the game. Is it because this is a game world so it's running on game logic? Will we see similar events that keep the in-world otome theme?

"What do you know about the 1st prince? He is rumored to attend," I ask.

"The 1st prince? He's missing."

"Not according to Lady Veronica. She said he's been in Rubar for 'peace talks' this whole time."

Maria sucks air sharply through her teeth. I can see she is thinking hard. "He's barely mentioned in the game and it clearly states he's been missing."

"In what context?"

"What do you mean?"

"How do you find out he has been missing? Does a character tell you?"

"Hmmm..... I'm pretty sure it's been mentioned in Prince Levi's route. But, I can't remember how you learn. I know Prince Levi doesn't mention it. He doesn't mention his brother at all. In fact, I don't think any of the capture targets do."

"So you learn this information incidentally somewhere else in the game." Maria nods. "Ok. Other than in-game, what do you know about him otherwise? You mentioned there's a rumor he is supposed to be one of the capture targets of the sequel.

"Yes. But it wasn't officially announced. So it was just rumors."

"But the game sequel was for sure coming out?"

"Yes. There was supposed to be a fan event, but I died before that happened."

"Let me think......." I say more for myself than for Maria. Let's assume the rumors are accurate and the 1st prince is one of the capture targets for the next game. Ok. I'm a game dev. How did this go down? Doki Doki Love Academy is released. Otome games are a dime a dozen and generally sell only to an established fan base. Most of those games don't even make it to the States.

Wait....

This one did. It was successful enough in Japan to warrant translation. Ok. So let's assume this is a particularly successful one. Actually. That's a fact. It's getting a sequel. What do sequels need to do? Unlike a movie, you can't just continue the story. The whole point of playing the game is to fall in love. You need new characters. But they have to anchor to the first game. Having a prince is almost a requirement for an otome game. AH HA!

"The 1st prince was never planned!" I say out loud.

"Huh?"

"Doki Doki Love Academy was never initially intended to have a sequel! So when it became successful enough for one they needed to find characters that would transition to the second game. They got lucky because, while Prince Levi is the crown prince, he isn't the only prince. What was intended as just a passing remark to give Levi backstory suddenly needed to become a fleshed-out character. Saying that he disappeared doesn't work for a continuation story. So let's assume Lady Veronica is correct and they changed his whereabouts to be in Rubar to tie him into the assassination storyline..."

"You don't think he's responsible for it?!" Maria exclaims.

"If this was an anime, I would totally think that. But he is supposed to be a capture target, so no. I don't think he is involved. I think the game devs needed to add a story in for the 1st prince, so they just fit him in where they could."

"Oh....OH!" Maria suddenly shouts. "What if The Handkerchief Contest is a game promo!!"

"A game promo?"

"Yes! They would release a promo about an event that has all the characters from both games. That way fans of the original can see their favorites interact with the new line up. Usually, this is done a few months before the official launch of the game."

"OH! You're right!! This event is supposed to have all the eligible unmarried men and women. There would be no other time during the events of the first game to host such an event because the capture targets start going their separate ways."

"How exciting! We are going to see the capture targets for the sequel!" Maria is bursting with fangirl energy.

"There's just one problem..... We don't know who any of the other capture targets are other than the 1st prince."

"Oh," she says sullenly. All the joy suddenly vanished. Ah, damn it. Depressed female protagonist is just too pathetic. No wonder the capture targets try so damn hard.

"Well, how about we have our own game then! Since this event doesn't impact your story at all, let's focus and try to guess who the next capture targets will be! We will make a list and someday we will start hearing about a girl with several men madly in love with her and we will know she is the new main character."

"I love that idea!!" Maria says with a little clap. "By the way, what kind of design are you thinking of making?"

"What do you mean?"

"For the embroidery on the handkerchief. I was thinking I'd do something with lilies!"

"Heh....eh...embroidery....right....." Do I know how to embroider??

Dear game kamisama, please send help!

Chapter 5 Part 3: A Contest of Wits

"I hope we're not too late," Maria said with concern as our carriage was very slowly making its way to the Imperial Gardens.

"I'm sorry, this is my fault."

"Oh no, I'm not blaming you. We knew we had to leave early to go by carriage. I just didn't think about the traffic jam to get in." Most everyone we knew was teleporting to the gardens. But not wanting to risk another bout of sickness, I had decided to go by carriage. I tried to persuade Maria to go before me, but she wouldn't leave me alone.

"How far away are we?" I ask.

"I don't very. But this line just isn't moving." Risking impropriety, I heave a sigh and open the carriage door. "Christine!!" Maria shouts with a startle.

"Relax, I'm just trying to see what's going on." I stand up to hang myself halfway out the door to try to gain an advantage to see ahead. We aren't all that far as I can see the gate. There is a checkpoint set there which explains the slowdown. Considering the size of the event it doesn't surprise me that security is tight. "We could walk to the gate from here," I shout back towards Maria. "The security checkpoint is bogging the whole thing down."

"WATCH IT!!" I hear a man shout. A carriage is barreling up the side quickly and I manage to haul myself back in before it takes my head off.

"HEY! YOU WATCH IT ASSHOLE!!" God, I always hated jerks who clearly see the lane is ending yet fly up the side to cut in line. I flick the carriage off for good measure.

No sooner than the carriage passes by but it comes to a sudden stop.

Shit.

I slam the door shut and sit down quickly.

"What's going on?" Maria askes me innocently.

"Ha. Ha. Nothing." I laugh nervously as I smooth my dress out. "We shouldn't stress it. We definitely will make it in time. After all, you're the protagonist. Even if this is an inconsequential promo event, it would never omit you."

Tap Tap

The rap on the door nearly makes me jump out of my seat.

"Is someone knocking on the door?"

"Just ignore it," I say nervously. Shit. Mr. Speedypants also has road rage.

Tap Tap

"It sounds like someone is there," Maria leans to open the door.

"NO! We don't know who it is?! Could be a kidnapper for all we know!" But Maria doesn't listen and opens the door. I swallow hard trying to steady my nerves. Who knows what kind of maniac I just pissed off.

"Chickadee!" I am greeted with a disgusting smile.

All my nerves float away instantly while I make my usual disgust noise upon seeing this annoying man.

"Duke Victor!" Maria exclaims in a sweet-sounding surprise. "Why are you knocking on our carriage door?"

"Well," he says as he enters and sits down next to me despite my lack of offer to do so. I maneuver myself into the opposite corner. "I needed to apologize to Lady Christine. My inattentive driver nearly caused an unfortunate accident." That shit-eating grin all over his face made it perfectly obvious he had heard my insults to his driver. "But perhaps I should give him a raise since it has allowed us to meet in such a serendipitous way." I roll my eyes.

"Are you on your way to the gardens as well?" Maria asks. I stare at her. Really? I know we are told there is no such thing as a stupid question. But that was a stupid question. Glancing at Duke Speedypants, I see he also has that same look questioning if her inquiry was serious.

"I think what Maria means, is that we are surprised to see you going to the gardens via carriage. I would have assumed you would have teleported in as that would be the less stressful means of transportation."

"Ah. I could have, yes. But I had a feeling that I would pick up some stray chicks if I went this way." In other words, he knew I couldn't teleport and Maria would accompany me by carriage. Damn capture target.

"Yes, I am forever doomed to arrive slowly. I thank you for your concern, but as you see I am completely unharmed. Please don't linger for our sakes."

He better not be thinking of sitting here with us the whole way in. Who knows how long that will be.

"Oh, I wasn't planning on lingering. I am a rather impatient person." Thank God for a small miracle. "But since we were able to meet in such a way you should accompany me!"

"What for?" I accidentally slip from my ladylike persona.

"You're very kind." It was Maria's turn to cover my blunder.

"Come now!" he grabs my hand and pulls me out of my seat.

"Now hold up a second!" I protest.

"I can get us past the guards much quicker. Get a move on ladies!"

"How fortunate!" Maria exclaims and pushes me gently out the door.

Resigned to our fate, I exit our carriage to enter the duke's instead. I make a point to make sure Maria and I sit next to each other so he can't weasel himself next to either of us.

It's annoying how nice his carriage is. Instantly my butt feels much better as the seating is well padded. The carriage is also more spacious than the public carriage we had hired. Victor sits down across from us with his wide playboy smile. I glance at Maria who is equally smiling dumbly. Tsk. Fine. Let the children grin like idiots at each other. Victor raps twice on the ceiling and the carriage moves forward.

"Thank you so much for your generosity," Maria says.

"No need to thank me. The pleasure is all mine."

"I was fearful we wouldn't make it and lose out from participating."

"I would never let that happen. Beautiful flowers belong in a garden."

"The weather is perfect for flower viewing! I hope we have enough time to see all the grounds," Maria says without catching the meaning of his comment.

"Even if there is a lack of time, you must see the gazebo in the western gardens. It is simply delightful at dusk and you both must make an effort to visit."

"Seeing the sunset must be very beautiful! Christine, we must make a note to see it!"

Is this conversation scripted? Not only is it the sappiest shit I have ever heard uttered with sincerity, but I am bored by its lack of actual content.

"Sure," I say deadpanned.

"Lady Christine, have you decided on a design for your handkerchief?" Victor asks me.

"Not really. Since I don't know what color I will end up with, I can't really plan for anything specific," I say with a shrug. Another small miracle, even though in my past life I had never learned embroidery, Lady Christine must-have. I found I had all the necessary muscle memory to not completely shame myself.

"Surely there is a color your aiming for."

"Not specifically."

"No need to be shy! All the ladies are strategizing what to pick. I would love to know."

"I have no such strategy."

"I'm aiming for something pink!" Maria interjects.

"How lovely! You should pick one that closely matches your hair. As for Lady Christine, might I suggest you select a purple handkerchief? I would complement your lovely eyes."

I shrug. "If the opportunity arises I'll consider it."

"Fantastic!" he exclaims with a clap.

The drive to the gardens felt even longer.

Chapter 5 part 4: A Contest of Wits

I really hated ditching Maria but I just couldn't stand to have any more of Duke Victor's conversation. Luckily the grounds were so packed and chaotic, I was able to slip away into the crowd. It's kinda a dick move, but I wasn't worried. Maria is the heroine. Even though I can't stand Duke Victor's personality, he is a capture target and will faithfully protect his heroine whether he realizes it or not. And even if Maria did manage to get into any trouble, one of the other capture targets would pop up. Even though I wouldn't mind taking the time to view the gardens, my current objective was to make it inside to the garden event hall. Why? To take this stupid hat off! I wore one out of obligation and can't politely take it off until I'm indoors somewhere. Then I can ditch this damn thing.

Weaving in out of the groups of people I hear bits of conversation. Groups of ladies trying to deduce what color a particular beau will pick. Young men of prominent standing toy with girls who are trying to learn what color they chose, while men of lesser standing practically calling out to any lady walking by to choose a particular color. As someone who never cared much for Valentine's Day, I was starting to regret ever saying anything bad about it. This was FAR more insane. Valentine's Day only meant something to already established couples (mostly). But since this was basically a giant matchmaking event, everyone was going all out.

Finally finding the entrance to the hall, I duck inside and quickly find the nearest servant to offload my hat. She hands me a tag so that I can reclaim my hat later. Typically my maid was supposed to take this, but I had run off on my own so I didn't have anyone with me. Oh well. I don't really care if I recover my stupid hat or not. I shove the ticket into my pockets. Yes. I have pockets. The first thing I did was have all my dresses fashioned with pockets. Lindsay was pretty horrified when I first brought it up, but she did what I asked. Then I started noticing that she also had pockets in her maid uniform.

Having made it safely to my goal, I finally have a chance to actually take in the sights. The hall was far less busy than outside. The ballroom was currently closed off. It was the largest room and was being prepared for the actual event. Duke Victor had graciously explained the process - one of the only times during the whole carriage ride that he said something worth paying attention to. The ladies go in and pick a handkerchief that has a number pinned to it. She gets a day to work on the design and tomorrow we bring them to the hunt. Before the hunt begins, the ladies try to find the suitor that matches the number. Easy enough, right? Wrong. Victor had mentioned when the doors open it's like the first charge of a battle. He said to not be surprised if there is kicking, pushing, hair pulling, and all-out fistfights to get to the tables first. And the kicker is that no one stops it. The men watch from the second level and cheer the women on like some kind of sporting event. Maria had asked if anyone had been injured but Victor had waved her off. No one would pull a weapon as that would get the guards' attention and come with, at best a hefty fine, at worst a prison sentence. As for the bruises, healers are standing by to flash those away quickly.

I started wandering the hallways where there were even fewer people. Mostly I passed servents. I found it exciting exploring the various rooms. Not that they had anything too particularly interesting, I fancied myself on a mini-adventure.

The fourth room I had poked my head into happens to have a lot of books so it gained my attention for further investigation. I walked to a random shelf to inspect what topics there might be.

The Voltare Horticulture Society Offical Handbook

The Gardener's Botanical

Medicinal Plants: Care and Usage

Fawna and Wildlife of the Northern Counties

The Complete Flower Companion

The Language of ---

"There isn't anything illuminating in this room, sadly," a voice said behind me. Jumping six inches in my skin, I let out a short screech.

I turn quickly and come face to face with, "Prince Levi!"

"Forgive me," he says chuckling slightly. "I didn't mean to frighten you."

"S-sorry," I say, my heart still racing. "If -- I'm just -- that is," I can't make a full sentence to save my life right now. I need to calm down. Taking a deep breath, I start again. "I didn't realize this room was in use. It wasn't my intention to pry. I won't intrude any more --"

"Please stay," he says cutting me off. "That is to say, I am not using this room in any official capacity, nearly as a respite."

"Ah," I say not knowing what to say. "It is a bit crazy out there," I add in hopes of sounding a bit more conversational. Even though I'm used to the prince going to the academy and I am used to Maria talking about her interactions with him, I, myself, have not had much reason to interact with him.

"You find me out."

"How so?"

"The attention that accompanies this event is not something I particularly relish," he says with a sign.

"Oh, I supposed being the number one capture target does have its disadvantages," I say with sympathy.

"Capture target?" he asks while cocking an eyebrow at me.

"Uh....heh...uh...."fuck fuck fuckity fuck.

He laughs. "How accurate. I suppose I am nothing more than prey at the mercy of a pack of hunters, or should I say, huntresses."

Thank God he has a sense of humor otherwise would I have been beheaded right there? I must do better. He's the crown prince. I have to set aside my modern sensibilities and remember that I can't speak to him as an equal.

"I have faith that you are a particularly resourceful prey and will emerge fairly unscathed."

"Indeed for opportunities present themselves at unexpected times," he says with a grin.

What dafaq does that mean? I was only extended the metaphor since I needed to keep it up to disguise my blunder, but now I'm totally lost. This kind of double talk - meaningless words with hidden meanings - is not my forte.

"Indeed," I opt for simple agreement.

An awkward silent moment passes. Am I suppose to keep the conversation going? What the hell am I suppose to say now? MARIA HELP ME!

A soft knock fills the room.

Omg! Did she use her heroine powers to come to save me?

The door opens and Sir Grey appears. "I'm sorry to disturb, Your Highness, but there are a few families we have yet to meet with."

"It looks likes my respite is over," he says offhandedly as he makes his way out of the room. "Oh Lady Christine," he stops before leaving.

"Y-yes?"

"May I recommend choosing a light pink handkerchief? I'm sure you would be able to create something quite lovely."

"Uh...I will certainly try."

With a bright smile, he leaves the room. Sir Grey pauses a moment to give me a small bow before leaving after him.

Chapter 6 Part 1: A Lady's War

Note from the author: Thank you everyone for your kind words. I've been super busy since the move and haven't had as much time to devote to this. I haven't dropped the story, just trying to manage my time. Thank you for hanging out with me and I hope you enjoy this update.

After enjoying a bit of a respite, the warning bell sounded indicating that the contestants should start gathering. Despite the massive crowd, I was surprised by how easily I was able to find Maria. Must be the power of the heroine to never get lost in a crowd. Maria was looking a bit nervous. I don't blame her, there were so many people packed in here it would be hard not to feel a bit overwhelmed.

"Hey!" I said as I tapped on her shoulder to get her attention.

"Christine!" she said happily with slight wetness to her eyes.

"Are you ok?"

"Yeah, there's just so many people here. It's worse than taking the train!" Train? Oh. That's right. I keep forgetting she's Japanese. From my fairly ignorant American point of view, I do know that Japanese teenagers have to sometimes take the train to get to school and that it can be ridiculously crowded.

"I guess so. Though I once went to a Metallica concert with my parents, and this reminds me of that."

"Ah....." she said noncommittally. I guess we both have unique perspectives that don't cross even our past lives' cultural boundaries.

"Oh before I forget," I say trying to change the mood, "I ran into," leaning down to whisper, "Prince Levi."

"You did?!" she asked wide eyed.

"Yeah. You need to pick a pink handkerchief!"

"Really? He told you that?"

"Yep. But, oh my God, I almost totally blew it!! I accidentally called him a capture target to his face!" Maria gasps out loud. I wave my hand to brush it off. "Don't worry! He thought I was making a joke so he laughed. But let me tell you, at that moment I knew true fear!" We both giggle at the absurdity of it.

Welcome, ladies! A loud voice booms in the air.

"Intercom?" I say with some confusion.

"It's wind magic," Maria tells me. "They can use it to amplify their voices."

"Ah, good thing you pay attention in class!"

"It wasn't mentioned in class yet. I was curious on how Lord Filmore is able to yell from across the grounds!" Lord Filmore isn't actually a lord. He's the school's groundskeeper. But he is old and cranky and has the respect of the teaching staff, so he was unofficially been called a Lord by the whole school for years. I haven't figured out why he can't actually get a title, I'm sure there's some bullshit about the aristocracy and him being a commoner.

As I am sure all of you are quite familiar with the event, please bear with me as there may be a few of you who need to hear the rules and proceedings.

Me. That would be me. I have no idea what's going to happen.

Momentarily you will be granted access to the hall where you will select only ONE handkerchief. As you are all ladies of class, I trust there will be NO pushing, shoving, or generally unbecoming behavior while entering the hall.

This comment resulted in a few snickers in the crowd. Well, it's pretty obvious that is exactly what is going to happen.

Clearing his throat, the unseen announcer continues. Once you have ORDERLY entered the hall and selected your desired handkerchief, we ask that you quickly leave and retreat to the gardens to allow the rest of the ladies to enter.

More snickering. What kind of bloodbath is this going to become?

After you have your handkerchief you are allowed the rest of the day to barter with another lady should you want to exchange, HOWEVER, once you have started on your designs OR leave the gardens, that handkerchief becomes your responsibility.

All handkerchiefs have a number tag. Remove the number tag and keep it safe. This will represent your partner during the exchange at the hunt next weekend.

The crowd erupts into loud chatter.

"There's a hunt too?" I ask Maria.

"I guess so. I really don't know anything about this either."

Quiet now! Quiet! Poor announcer. It's like the principal trying to calm a student body before a pep rally. And finally, I am sad to announce that this year there are more ladies participating than gentlemen. Some of you will not be able to get a handkerchief. If that is the case, you will receive a special invitation to the next Handkerchief Contest in which you will be among the first to enter.

Now the crowd becomes hysterical. Lovely, not enough for everyone to participate truly means a blood bath. Maybe I should just hang back. Is this really worth it?

The doors are opening, please REMAIN CALM!!

No sooner than he speaks the doors open and the crowd surges forward. While I was entertaining the idea of skipping, it was no longer a reality I could choose from. I was being pushed and elbowed forward and it would be suicide to attempt to move in any other direction. I lost Maria to the crowd quickly.

"Ah - shit!" I put my arms up to protect my head. There are girls pulling hair and using their long fingernails to scratch people out of the way. I can't see where I'm going. And my head is ringing. The screams of excitement, hysteria, and pain are so loud and high pitched it hurts. I remember I had this friend who really liked Taylor Swift. She would post-concert videos on Facebook and I remember I could barely hear the song over the screaming. This was that same hell.

Metal fans are waaaaaay nicer!

Eventually, I'm pushing hard into a table hitting my hip bone. "AH! FUCK Jesus!" There are handkerchiefs on this table so without looking I just grab one to try to make my retreat.

"Fuck this shit. Fuck. Fuck. Fuck." I mutter as I push my way out of the hall, which is slightly easier than getting in. Once I gain a bit of room to move without running into bodies and skirts, I run out the door into the gardens and don't look back. The adrenaline is surging and I'm in complete flight mode. Once the noise fades to the background, I finally stop and sit down at the closest bench heaving heavily.

"I. am. NEVER. doing this bullshit again!" I say to no one.

I lean back and stare at the sky. The breeze feels nice. Once I catch my breath I realize I have a death grip on the handkerchief in my hand. I look down. Releasing my gasp slightly I see a black cloth.

"Ha! Hahahahahahaha," I'm laughing like I'm insane. Tears are rolling down my eyes from laughing so hard. Once I get it out of my system I lean back again, the sky inviting me. Ah, truly fuck this shit.

Chapter 6 Part 2: A Lady's War

I didn't move. I didn't want to. I don't even know how much time had passed. I stopped staring at the sky once the sounds had died to almost nothing. I couldn't see the hall from where I was and eventually all I could hear were the birds chirping in the nearby tree. All my energy was gone. Physically I felt like I had been beaten up, I ached and there were a few spots I could feel the bruises already forming. My arms had welts from what I can only assume was nail scratches. Mentally, I was defeated. I couldn't handle the chaos inside the building but then I find I had picked the one handkerchief everyone told me to avoid.

I heard footsteps approaching from behind me, but I was so disassociated from my surrounding it barely registered.

"---stine?"

...

"Lady Christine? Are you alright?" someone asked while taking a seat next to me.

"Yes......no. Eh, sorta." I feel a warm magic spread over me and I close my eyes. Ahhhh, this feels good. The soreness and stinging vanishes. The relief washes over me and I feel the haze in my mind start to clear up. Healing magic. I haven't really experienced it yet. "Thank you." I turn to address my hero.

"I am always happy to help a student. Although, I am surprised how easily you absorbed my magic. I could have downranked the spell far lower still."

I blink at him a few times while staring at his messy brown hair. "Oh, Professor! I didn't realize it was you." I'm too tired (and grateful) to mind his presence right now.

Chuckling slightly he says, "No I did not think you did. I've seen that look before...." he trails off.

"What kind of look?" I'm suddenly self-conscious of how I might appear. I touch my hair, I'm sure it's a disaster.

"It's the look many soldiers have after a battle," he says with no humor in his voice. "When your senses have failed and the only thing left is your mind - but just barely so."

I say nothing. What could I say? It's not like I've seen war or real bloodshed. I remember Maria mentioning something about him being in a war. A long silent moment falls between us and I find I have no desire to fill it.

I wonder how Maria did. I've always envisioned her as more delicate than I am. Would the heroine plot armor keep her safe?

"Anything you design will be grand in the Duke's eyes," Professor McGreggor says breaking the silence. I look down at the handkerchief in my hand. It's supposed to be anonymous, and instead, I'm entirely aware of who my partner is.

"Do you know him, Professor?"

"Yes. Ellis and I go back a while.

"What's he like?"

"You mean to know if he is as ruthless as the rumors," he says coldly.

"No. That's not it. It's just -" I sigh. "It's just - I realize that rumors can create prejudice. I admit that I am not so unaffected by them. But of all the people I have heard talk about him, none of them have said they know him. So I suppose, as someone who actually knows what kind of man he is, what advice can you give me? Is he quick to offend? Are there things I should be cautious about? That sort of thing, if that makes sense."

"You're quite mature for your age," he comments. Obviously. "There are few who would even attempt to learn beyond what they see. As for Ellis, it is a complicated question as he is a complicated man. The rumors are not all baseless, but they lack context. He is an extraordinary champion. When they call him a demon on the battlefield, there really isn't any other way to describe it. If you hear stories about his feats, even if exaggerated, it would still be within his ability. War is brutal and unforgiving. And in a way, so is Ellis."

"But you say this without fear."

"Because I am fortunate to not be a target at the end of his blade. But, to answer your question, he is not all savage and war. He's a fair man and manages his estates and lands with a level hand. The people who live under him do not suffer needlessly. He cares a great deal about the common folk and makes decisions that benefit the majority, even at loss to himself. He's extremely loyal. If he considers you a friend, you will have his friendship to the hells and back. Of course," he laughs, "if you are an enemy he will drag you to the hells and back too!"

I chuckle with him.

"I applaud you for trying to keep an open mind and entice you to continue to do so until you can make your own judgments."

"Thank you, I will try." I look at the black cloth again. "But why black? That certainly doesn't help his reputation."

"I asked him that a long time ago, and you know what he said?"

I shake my head slightly.

"Blood doesn't show on black."

Chapter 6 Part 3: A Lady's War

"Yo! Alan!"

I hear someone call out for the professor. Looking to the side I see a man gracefully striding over to us. He defiantly has an air of confidence you can see right away. His blond hair is braided intricately and tied up in the back with adornments of various colors of glass beads. He was also sporting a well-groomed five o'clock shadow.

"Your highness," Professor McGreggor stands and bows slightly. Your highness? Who is he? Not wishing to offend whoever this is, I stand and mirror the professor's bow.

"Oh ho, what's this? Why you sly dog, I didn't know you had any game with the ladies, let alone attractive ones." The unidentified royal grabs my hand to place a light kiss on the top. Gross. I still don't like men randomly leaving their saliva all over my hands. I was unconsciously wiping the top of my hand on my dress, which he noticed before I knew what I was doing. Whoops!

"She is a student, Claude."

Is Professor Pedophile actually making that distinction?

"Still a lovely flower either way. And may I inquire on the lady's name? Or do students not have names?" he says with a playful tone.

Clearing my throat I introduce myself. "I am Lady Christine Eldergast, your highness."

"Eldergast? Hmmmm....." he thinks for a moment. "Ah! Any relation to Earl Eldergast?"

"Yes, he is my father."

"Smashing!" he says with a wide smile and a twinkle in his blue eyes. Is he wearing eyeliner? It sure looks like he is. "So what are you doing hanging out with this old man instead of entertaining much more interesting company?"

"I needed a respite from the chaos of the handkerchief selection and the professor happened upon me and provided a much-needed healing spell."

"You healed her?" he said with mocking sarcasm.

"Relax, it was a very minor spell," Professor McGreggor informed him.

"Oh!" the still-unnamed man exclaims as he notices the handkerchief in my hand. "You got Ellis!"

"Yes."

"Can you do me a favor?"

"Well, it depends if it's something within my ability."

"Can you embroider a giant penis on his handkerchief?"

"CLAUDE!!" Professor McGreggor shouts.

"Seriously! The biggest, erect penis you can."

"Claude, this is NOT appropriate!"

"And may I ask why I should risk offending the duke with a giant, erect penis?" I ask him with humor in my voice.

"So that he knows how big of a DICK he is!"

"CLAUDE, enough." The professor's warnings are obviously falling on deaf ears. "Besides, the young lady is not likely knowledgable to... such things." Oh, really? What are you implying? While I'm sure the original owner of this body wouldn't have, I am not so innocent. This - Claude - seems to have a sense of humor, so I decided to push it a bit.

"Well if anyone wants to volunteer as a model for reference, I can make arrangements." My comment makes the professor groan while Claude's eyes light up it merriment.

"Absolutely! I would be happy to show you now if you'd like."

"Forgive me, I left my magnifying glass at home."

Claude erupts in contagious laughter. My joke was pretty lame - the kind of insult you would hear 13-year-old boys making. But he was laughing so heartily I couldn't help but join in. Meanwhile, the professor is holding his head in shame.

"I like you!" Claude says giving me a slight slap on the shoulder.

"I implore you, please steer this conversation back to something more appropriate," Professor McGreggor pleas while looking directly at me. Fine fine. I guess he did compliment my maturity a bit ago and here I am completely destroying it.

"I will take your - request - into consideration. But if I do make such a risk, who may I tell the duke is responsible so I can direct his wrath elsewhere."

"Ah, I am happy to take full responsibility. I am Prince Claude Theodis Sunspire, eldest born to King Alfonse Rubia Sunspire and Queen Elina Sunspire," he says with a sweeping bow. "And don't worry. Ellis and I are close friends. He will let me off easily."

Professor McGreggor snorts. "Sure. He will easily toss you through a window."

"Oh come now, Alan. He's quite the gentle giant," Prince Claude says to me with a wink. I catch Professor McGreggor rolling his eyes.

"Brother!"

Prince Claude looks past me. "YO! Little bro!" he calls out waving his arm. I turn to see Prince Levi and Sir Grey approaching.

"Greetings to -" Claude pushes past me interrupting my greetings and grabs Levi in a bear hug. Right siblings. It seems as though Claude has forgotten any commitment to his prior conversation and starts pulling Levi away by the shoulders while Levi struggles to separate himself.

"Lady Christine, please forgive the first prince's rudeness," Sir Grey says to me.

"It's ok. I conversed with him enough to gather he isn't one to stand on protocol."

"Pssh. An understatement," Professor McGreggor chimes in.

"I'm glad to see that they have a warm relationship," I comment. This is a good opportunity to see if there is any bad blood about Claude being skipped for the crown.

"There is no loss of affection," Sir Grey replies tactfully. Fine. Don't give me any juicy gossip. "Oh, my lady, I saw Lady Maria not long ago. She was looking for you. You may want to seek her out, she seemed a bit distraught."

"Oh, thank you, Sir Grey. I best be off. Professor," I turn to address the man. "Thank you for your company."

"Of course, anytime."

Chapter 6 Part 4: A Lady's War

Luckily Maria was right where Sir Grey said she would be. The gardens had gotten incredibly congested as large groups lingered to talk about the events. I noticed laughter and crying, indifference, and villainous staring. I hadn't run into Lady Veronica yet, which was a small blessing. Maria and I made eye contact and she quickly walked over to me. She grabbed my arm tightly.

"We need to go," she hissed quietly.

"Huh? Why?" she started dragging me along. "Are you hurt?"

"No. No. It's just - it's better if we leave." I noticed she seemed pretty shaken up. Considering what I went through, I can't argue any. Maybe as the heroine, she had a worse experience.

"Ok, I trust you. I wasn't particularly having that great of a time myself." She nodded half hearing while we crossed the grounds at a rapid pace aiming for the area the carriages would make their pick-ups. As we walked briskly, someone snuck into my blind spot and matched pace with us.

"You're walking fast," a soft voice commented. Recognizing the voice, but turning back to confirm my suspicions, I see Simon a step behind.

"Ah Simon - Maria slow down just a tad - how are you? We are just on our way out," I said over my shoulder.

"It's early," he commented.

"True. But it was very tiring."

"Oh no!" Maria suddenly stops.

"What?" I ask.

"This way." She yanks me to the side and starts walking in a different direction. Simon is following like a confused puppy.

"Seriously Maria, what is it?"

...

She was focused on a new direction, which for some reason was making me a little nervous. If we are leaving, but have no abandoned the carriages, then the only other way out would be to teleport. Rounding the corner we almost slam into someone.

"Oh my! I'm sorry," I hastily apologize. A kid, maybe around 12 or 13 folds his arms and stares us down.

"You!" he says pointing at Maria. "Why are you avoiding me?"

"I - I- I'm not avoiding you," she says with fear in her voice. I step in front of Maria to offer what little protection I can.

"Look, kid. My friend isn't feeling well, and we are in a hurry to get home so she can rest."

"Kid?!" he practically spits out the word, his amber eyes not hiding his arrogance.

"Yes, kid," I emphasize the word knowing it would piss him off. In reality, I should be more mindful of not pissing off some brat kid of a powerful Duke or something. But I really don't care. Maria has heroine power. If things got nasty with this kid, one of the capture targets would swoop down and save her. Having Simon in tow was insurance. Granted he has been pretty soft-spoken the whole time I've known him, but perhaps the heroine in danger will awaken his main character powers. I see the kid literally take a big breath in ready to launch into whatever temper tantrum he was about to have. I decide to cut him off before this happens.

"Pardon our rudeness, I'll buy you a cookie or something if we ever meet again. Later!" I grab Maria's hand and start running in the direction she was initially steering me towards. We run through the meandering crowds not caring how inappropriate it looked.

"Left," Maria calls out and we turn. Off to the side, I happen to make eye contact with Prince Claude, who is surrounded by a few other gentlemen. He gives me a big smile and waves from afar.

"What a cheeky bastard," I say under my breath.

"What?" Maria asks.

"I'll tell you when we get back. Are we close?" I say slowing down now that there are fewer people around.

"Uh.... I think so."

"Are you teleporting?" I look back and Simon apparently had decided to keep up with us. Aw, such a good puppy.

"Yes, do you know where it is? We arrived by carriage so we didn't see the teleporter." I ask him.

He nods and takes the lead. Maria and I follow in silence. What is going on? I look at her pale face. After a moment we arrive at the teleportation circle. I stare at it with an obvious frown on my face. Today is not a good day. Not only did I get beaten up, but I also grab the worst handkerchief I could, and now I am destined to end the day with my stomach in knots.

"It makes you sick, right?" Simon asks me with puppy dog eyes.

"Yeah," I tried to act nonchalant about it. "It's ok. Maria needs to get back, so I can endure it."

"Here." He reaches into his pocket and hands me a vial with a dark green liquid in it. I hesitate about taking it. "It's for teleportation sickness. You need it."

"Oh!" I said as I take it from him. Come to think of it, last time I was so sick I drank the vial without so much as glancing at it. "Thank you, Simon, that's really kind of you. But won't you need it?"

"Me?"

"Yeah. If I take it, then what about yourself?"

"I don't get sick."

"Ah," I say like I totally understand what he's saying. Why would he be randomly carrying this around if he didn't need it? But I don't feel like prying the information out of him and want to get Maria back so I leave it for now. "Maria, you good to go?" I ask to make sure.

"Yeah. Thanks, Simon."

We step into the circle and tense up in anticipation of what is to come.

The second time teleporting, while uncomfortable, wasn't nearly as gut-wrenching. I still don't feel that great after we arrive and quickly down the vial to settle my stomach. Maria supports me as we walk slowly back to our room. Though we both arrived looking like ghosts, by the time we got back the color had returned to both of our faces.

"So....." I say as I fall into the sofa. "Spit it out. Because I deserve a damn good explanation as to why I had to use that blasted teleporter."

"I know. I'm sorry. But -" she sighs. "It was the secret character."

"Oh?" I sit up a little straighter. She had told me about the existence of the secret character but never told me any details since she didn't like him. "Well, you have to tell me about him! Even if you don't like him."

"I know......"

Doki Doki Magic Love Academy: The Secret Character

S alvus Neverwood, High King of the Woodland Fae

Fae? Like fairies? With wings?

"Yeah basically."

Woah. I didn't realize there were non-humans here.

"There aren't many from what I understand."

Age: unknown, but no less than a couple thousand years

Is he immortal?

"Dunno. The game never really said if he was."

Blood Type: KX

What the hell does that mean?

"He's not human, so he doesn't have human blood. In the game when he is injured, his blood is blue."

Oh, cool.

Magical Affinity: Verdant and Fae

You haven't said what he looks like.

"Well... you saw him."

I did? When?

"He was the one you called kid."

What?! He was like 12!

Appearance: teal green hair and amber eyes.

"There's more to this. I'll explain."

Backstory: The fae have been hidden for hundreds of years as their relationship with humans was never the best. The king starts to get bored and decides to watch humans, and he happens to decide to watch the Academy. He becomes interested in human magic and how they are teaching, so he pretends to be a human to enroll. Since he hasn't been around humans in a long time, he misjudges what age the students are and transforms into a 13-year-old boy. He uses fae magic to charm the headmaster and he's admitted as a prodigy student.

Ok. So this is pretty typical. A non-human learning what it's like to be human then falling in love with a human.

"The setup is."

Since he is a special character, you can only trigger him with the following conditions: First, you had to complete the game with any other character first. Second, by the end of your first year, if you did not gain enough relationship points to have any of the capture targets ask you to the end of year ball, then he will appear the following semester.

Wait. I thought the end of year ball happens at the end of the second year.

"No, it's the end of year ball because it happens at the end of each year. As first years, it is just a CG event for the capture target you have the highest relationship with."

Ok. But why do you hate this guy? Other than, he obviously is a little shit.

To get Salvus' good ending, you have to focus solely on raising his relationship stats. Since you only have half the game, you have to ignore everything else that happens including the assassination plot. If you succeed he whisks you away to be his bride to live in the fairy realm. But since you didn't interact with the other capture targets, you essentially get the bad endings of all the other characters simultaneously. Prince Levi is killed, Sir Grey loses his whole family, Lord Simon marries Lady Angelica, Professor McGreggor never regains his magic ability, and Duke Victor will remain a good for nothing playboy. It's also alluded that Rubar eventually invades the kingdom and institute a reign of tyranny.

Jesus. This is the good ending??

To get Salvus' bad ending, you don't romance him after he enters the academy. This means even if you manage to max out your skills for another capture target, since he is present, he will automatically override that ending. He decides that humans are weak and pathetic and have no redeeming qualities and this whole thing was a waste of his time. But since the heroine was the person who initially grabbed his attention, he decides to kidnap her and bring her back to the fairy realm where she is treated like a court jester - a plaything to keep the king amused.

WTF. Both his endings suck!!

"To be honest, when I played the game I didn't mind him. But once we were reincarnated here, and I realized that all these people are real people, I couldn't imaging picking a route that ends in the worst possible way for everyone."

I totally support that. But you know what this means?

"What?"

You need a date to that damn ball! No matter what!

Chapter 7 Part 1: Life Path Unlocked

"By the way, what color handkerchief did you get?" I ask Maria.

"Oh! Look!" she pulls out a light pink handkerchief from her pocket.

"That's definitely Prince Levi's," I comment.

"You can't be sure of that!"

"Ah, yes I can. One: he told me to choose a pink handkerchief. Two: You're the heroine. There is no possible way for you to not pick a capture target."

Maria pouts a little. "Ok, I guess you're right. But I wanted a pink one even before you told me!"

"Yeah, that doesn't matter. Destiney is holding your hand."

"What about you?"

"Heh....Well about that....." I grab the black handkerchief I've been burdened with.

"Oh!" Maria looks at it wide-eyed not saying anything more.

"Yeah, bad luck I know."

"What are you going to do?" she askes me concerned.

"Well not stress it. I ran into Professor McGreggor and he reassured me that Archduke Wintergard is a reasonable man. I should be ok as long as I don't piss him off - oh! speaking of which - I met the first prince!"

"Really?! What is he like?"

"Cheerful and cheeky. He has an affable sense of humor." I purposely omit telling Maria about his request. While I was happy enough to play along in the moment, I am not embroidering a penis on his handkerchief.

"Did you meet anyone else who might be capture targets for the sequel?"

"No. I only ran into the Professor, Prince Levi, and Sir Grey briefly. I was mostly hiding from the chaos."

"Bummer. I am really curious about who they might be!"

"Me too. But we may still have our chance at the hunt. They will have to be there, and since it shouldn't be as insane, it would be a better opportunity to do some reconnaissance." Maria nods along in agreement. "Although, I could use your help."

"Sure. For what?"

"I have no idea what to design! While I was pleasantly surprised I actually could embroider, I don't want to bite off more than I can chew. Plus, since the Archduke is an elite noble, I need to give at least a certain amount of effort."

"Oh.....right. He doesn't seem like the kind of person standard floral designs would be appropriate for." We both sit in silence while we think. "What do you know about him?"

I go over my conversation with Profesor McGreggor in my head and I realize I didn't really gain much information. "Nothing. I only know the obvious. He's a warrior of great talent and he's from the north. That's it."

"What about checking the library tomorrow? We can find some books about the northern territories and see if there is any inspiration."

"That's a good idea. I don't think we should rule out flowers, but use them in conjunction with something else. Hmmmmm, maybe like an animal or a famous landmark?"

"A landmark?" Maria asks obviously confused.

"Yeah. For example, if someone said he was from Paris, I could put the Eiffel Tower on it. Or like you're from Japan, so Mount Fuji."

"Ah! Statue of Liberty!"

"Right!" I snap my fingers at her. "It might be a little generic, but could work."

"No, it's a good idea! I don't think I've seen buildings or mountains used in handkerchief designs since I've been here. We may think it's generic because where we are from that kind of picture is all over tourist areas, but it might be a new idea here."

"Good point! Ha! I almost forgot we can freely rob ideas from our past lives!"

"Yep! There is a lot of manga in Japan where that exact thing happens. Sometimes they build business empires and stuff!"

"Well, I doubt I have the skill or knowledge to become a business tycoon, that's a little extreme. But where I may lack in refinement I can make up for in ingenuity!"

Despite having an exhausting weekend, I was able to wake up feeling refreshed and attend classes without much trouble. Which is more than I can say for most of the girls I ran into. The ones in Maria and my general studies class looked completely devastated. It was obvious they did not get much sleep. Even Maria seemed more lethargic than usual. My second class for the day was what I was more interested in, or rather not the class, but having a chance to speak to Professor McGreggor again. I had a mission to glean a bit more information from him this time. I took my seat next to the window as usual and moments before becoming late, Duke Victor slides into the seat next to me. While I've gotten used to him slipping in last minute, it annoys me that he won't sit next to any one of his adoring fans AND that he has to pester me all throughout class.

"Chickadee! I heard a rumor -" "It's likely true," I cut him off. "Please be quiet."

"But how did you know what I was going to say?" he askes with mock offense.

"I don't live a scandalous life, unlike some people, so it's not hard to guess what the content of this rumor is."

"So sad. I gave you a perfectly fine recommendation and yet you snub me so decidedly!" He says with the timbre of a very bad actor while placing his hand over his heart. I give him, what could only be called, the bitch please face.

"Recommendation or not, I didn't have the luxury of choosing. I just grabbed and ran. Had I known what to expect, I would have suited up in full armor instead of a dress!"

"Ha!" Duke Victor lets out a bark. "Now THAT I would LOVE to see!"

"I know everyone had an exciting weekend, but please let's focus on class now," Professor McGreggor speaks up to get everyone's attention. I have to admit I did form too strong a prejudice against him at first. While I am not excited by the prospect that a 30-year-old man would "fall in love" with a teenager, he hasn't shown any predilection of it being a pattern. And he is is a pretty good educator. He has just enough sternness in his voice to calm the class down and get them focused on class, but not so much so that he becomes a tyrant teacher. It's a fine balance that only great teachers master. He even manages to command enough respect that Duke Victor stays mostly quiet. Although that doesn't mean he doesn't attempt to annoy me in other juvenile ways.

"Don't worry, I am not here to dampen your spirits, but rather to carry forward the excitement. Today we are going to performing practical spell-work." Excited murmurs and clapping erupt.

PRACTICAL?! Like DOING magic?! We've spent the first few weeks just learning out of the textbook.

Chuckling slightly Professor McGreggor continues. "Open your books to page 28. We are going to start with elemental summoning. Each year a few students find out their elemental affinity when tasked with using magic for the first time. So I am very excited to see what kind of results we have this year!"

Ah heck yeah!

Chapter 7 Part 2: Life Path Unlocked

"Seriously, Chickadee! That is too much!" Duke Victor laughed as he shielded his eyes.

"Ha ha! Admit defeat and I will not turn you into a pathetic blind man!" I say as I wield light magic from my palm pointed at his obnoxious face.

"Never!" he said as he misted water into my face. The front of my bangs and the top of my uniform was completely drenched as we had been attacking each other for the past 10 mins. Once we had learned how to do a basic summon with all the elements, we were allowed to practice with our seat partners. It didn't take long for us to start using it as very weak, sad weapons. Although in my defense, Duke Victor started it first by blasting me with wind magic. To his credit, Professor McGreggor was allowing controlled chaos in his class. He was walking around giving a few tips here and there but generally allowing the students to enjoy their first day of actual spellcasting. The bell sounded signaling the end of class which halted everyone pretty quickly.

"Ah sad," I said. "I suppose today I will have to be satisfied with a stalemate."

"Indeed!" Duke Victor started to get up and blasted me with warm wind before buggering off. I'm a little irritated he was able to mix fire and wind so quickly. Since he doesn't bring anything to class he was able to slip out as quickly as he is late to arrive. I, on the other hand, had my stuff scattered all over the desk as our battle had caused all my belongings to become casualties of war. As I was packing my belongings, Professor McGreggor approached me.

"Lady Christine, I was wondering if you would spare me a moment of your time."

"Huh? Sure," I said as I slowed down grabbing my things.

"Have you tested for your affinity yet?"

"Eh.... no."

"I think you should."

"Why? Isn't it still pretty early in the year? I thought most people would start to feel a leaning towards an element." Excluding Maria who was a heroine weirdo, most people needed to start with very basic magic to learn what element they were naturally gifted in.

"True. But I wasn't lying when I said that many students find their affinity during this very lesson. I noticed your light magic was particularly stronger."

"My light magic? That was nothing! I was just trying to be a jerk to Duke Victor."

"May I ask - and I will not reprimand you for having ill intentions - what were you thinking while casting?"

"What was I thinking?" I paused a moment. "Well I suppose, how do I get back at this jerk."

"But your light magic got stronger as you were practicing. So what did you think when you did that?"

To be honest, the first thing I thought was how my palm looked like a personal flashlight. So I just kept trying to my 'flashlight' brighter. But flashlights don't exist here, so I need to figure out how to explain that. "I guess I just thought about trying to get it as bright as possible……like…… like the sun! You can't look at the sun because it's blinding. So I wanted it to be like that!" I said proudly.

"I see," he said as he drummed his chin. "So in other words, you focused on the element and used your mana to intensify the effect."

"I suppose. Sounds like the most accurate clinical evaluation you could have."

"I think you should get tested. I have a strong feeling you're a light magic-user."

"Heh?! L-light magic-user?!" The alarm bells were going off in my head.

"Yes. It takes a certain amount of natural ability to strengthen a skill with no training. Within minutes you had already doubled the luminosity of your spell with little effort. That leads me to conclude that you have a natural light magic inclination. Which is great news! Healers are well respected and Lord knows we always could use more!" he said with obvious joy.

"Now wait a minute. One flashlight spell does not make me a light magic-user."

"Flashlight?"

"And I don't have any inclinations to be a healer."

"It's not a matter of inclination. If you have the talent, it's a duty to become a healer."

"NO!" I said forcefully taking the Professor by surprise. "I am not a healer." I grabbed my bag and fled the room as fast as I could.

A healer?! Ha. No way! There was something churning inside of me that was strongly against the idea. While I wouldn't be so unkind to say the idea was repulsive, I definitely feel some indignity with the mere idea I would be a healer. To be honest, I never even gave the healing profession a passing thought. The only reason I was against Maria becoming a light magic-user was that I wanted to keep her away from an inappropriate romance. But it's not like I had any strong feelings against healers - or so I thought.

"I need to find Maria," I said out loud and to no one. I made my way to the dining hall as fast as I could speed walk. Maria is the expert of this game world. She knows all about the original Christine Eldergast. She should tell me what magic I am supposed to have. I can't believe I didn't think to ask her this before.

I entered the dining hall and scanned the room for pink hair. I didn't see her, but noticed Simon in our usual spot so I made my way over to him.

"Hey, Simon," I greeted him informally while sitting down heavily. "Have you seen Maria yet?"

"No," he said quietly. From the looks of things, he had already ordered tea for the three of us as the cups were already present.

"I guess she's running late," I sighed as I poured the tea for myself. The bright red liquid fills my cup. "Figures. The one day I have a lot to vent about....."

"I can help?" he said sounding like an undecided mix of a question and a statement.

"It's - nothing you can help with." I notice the dejected puppy dog look in his face. "Don't worry! It's just....girl...stuff."

"Girl stuff?" he asked innocently.

"Yeah, stuff only other girls would understand. I'm sure there are boy things that you wouldn't ask me and Maria about. Something like that." Blowing on the teacup, I move to take a sip. It smells like hibiscus today. The scent already starts to relax me.

"Ah. Like sex stuff."

I both snort and spit the tea with his comment. "Ah shit. Sorry. Sorry." I say using the napkin to clean up. My innocent cinnamon roll completely took me by surprise with that comment. Deciding it best to ignore his comment, I try to change topics. "Have you ordered yet?"

"No."

"Ah heh. Let's order! It will be Maria's punishment for being late." I flag down a waiter. After placing our orders, I scan the room again. It's not like her to be this late for lunch.

Tsk. "It's frustrating not having a cell phone! Freaking text me if your held up."

"What's a cell phone?"

"Cell phone.....eh... " I think about how to explain my blunder. "You know the message stations?" Simon nods. "A cell phone is a small message station. Small enough to fit in your hand! And you carry it around. So you can get your messages anywhere anytime. So I would message Maria Where are you? And she would message back Stuck in class or not feeling good or on my way now! Then we would both know if we should wait or not, or be worried or not."

"Ah." Simon says nodding away deep in thought. I really should be more careful about my modern language. I've been messing up more and more and it's becoming too much of a habit. What if someone discovers I'm not the real Christine. Isn't it the trope in these isekai stories for the big reveal to be some sort of taboo? Like I'd pegged as a witch. Wait. This world already has magic. What would be the magical world equivalent of a witch? Death Eater? Yeah, they would treat me like they uncovered a secret Death Eater. Off to Doki Doki Azkaban I go!

Chapter 7 Part 3: Life Path Unlocked

"Eldergast!" Sir Sizemore barks at me.

"Y-yes?!" I freeze in place. Sir Sizemore walks over to me and slaps me on the back.

"I think we finally found a weapon that suits you!"

"Really?!" I ask with excitement. I'm currently holding a short sword. I had hoped I had some talent with the short sword so I could have an excuse to keep the one I won from the Combat Wizards tourny I entered.

"About time too. I was worried you'd end up like those other useless women who only use staves as walking sticks."

"That's a bit mean, sir."

"Heh like I care. They aren't my students! McGreggor can keep the fat and flabby all to himself." I grimace. He lacks tact. Although this might be as much tact as one can expect from a military veteran. Sir Sizemore was a commoner that rose through the ranks over the years of service. He didn't have the same educational background as the aristocracy. And if the movies depicting how a bunch of military dudes talking with each other is to be believed, then I suppose this might be tactful all things considering. "So are the rumors of you having a Dragon Scale sword true?"

"Ah, yes! How did you know?"

"Sir Grey. He commented on how he was jealous of it. I can't see why though. He uses longswords."

"I'd wager it was mostly jealousy regarding the nature in which I acquired it. Getting something for free is always better than paying for the exact same item!"

"Ha. No truer words can be spoken!" Sir Sizemore bellowed heartily. "20 more strikes on the dummy and you can finish up for the day."

"Yes, sir!"

"And watch your arm! Don't let it sag!"

"Y-yes, sir!"

After combat basics, I headed to the room to bathe. I got especially sweaty today and knew Maria wouldn't be back for a bit as she had mentoring sessions with Simon. Since she didn't show up to lunch, I told Simon to let her know not to dawdle on her way back today. The bath that Lindsay drew up felt extra good today. She added a bit of lavender to help me relax. It had been fairly stressful lately. The weekend killed me with the whole black handkerchief thing - ah shit, I just remembered I never ended up asking Professor McGreggor for more information about the archduke's lands. And speaking of the Professor, the mentioning of light magic really makes my skin crawl. Then Maria skips lunch and I pound out my aggressions on a straw dummy. I'm sure my arm is going to sore later.

After my bath, I ask Emily to prepare some tea and snacks. Maria should be back soon, and if she missed lunch, she will likely need something to hold her over until dinner.

"Miss, you have a guest," Emily has returned no sooner than she had left.

"Me? Now? Why didn't they just knock?"

"Well miss, it's a gentleman. He can't enter the dorms without an escort."

"Oh. Who is it?"

"Lord Simon Clark."

"Simon? Why isn't Maria with him then? Nevermind. I'll go find out." I head out of the room to meet Simon at the entrance.

"Simon!" I greet him. "Why isn't -""Maria never came to class," he interrupts me.

"What do you mean?" I ask worried now.

"She never showed up. I waited till the end."

"Shit. I don't like this. Skipping lunch is one thing, but she would never skip class! Did you happen to see her at all today?" He shakes his head. I figured it was unlikely. Maria's entire day revolves around giving all the capture targets equal opportunity to spend time with her, even if they themselves are not aware of it. "Ok. We have to think of where she might be......." I start to pace while recalling our conversations. Nothing out of the ordinary happened this morning. We both got ready and had breakfast like normal. Last night we spoke about the secret character and speculated about the archduke. Oh, she mentioned the library. We were going to do research there. But - that doesn't seem likely. Missing lunch to go to the library might be possible, but also missing class - that's not like Maria. But I also don't want to completely disregard the possibility.

"Hey Simon, can you do me a favor?"

"Yes."

"Maria and I talked about doing some research in the library. Though we didn't make any solid plans, do you mind checking just in case she's there? And if you do find her, give her a scolding for making her friends worry!"

"Yes," and with little ceremony, Simon walks away quickly.

He's not likely to find her there. Ok, let's think about this. Maria is the heroine. What happens to heroines? They get bullied. Lady Angelica probably did - THAT'S IT! Maria is probably in some sort of slight danger because of Lady Angelica. What happens in these types of stories? Let's see there is:

gang of girls cornering the heroine and being mean and/or physically violenthmm, not likely she would miss more than just lunch

Stealing her clothes while changing forcing her to hide in the changing roomshe has combat basics before me, I would have seen her when I went to class

Tricking her to go somewhere and getting kidnappeda possibility, but seems like more an end game tatic

Locking her in an empty roomvery high probability

Trapping her on the roofbuildings here are fairly short, but also could be a possibility

Out of all of these, being locked in a room is the most likely scenario. Now how do I go about this? I doubt Lady Angelica would tell me the truth, so there is no reason to even speak to her. And I am still under her radar, and I would like to keep it that way as long as possible. What would the game do? The heroine is trapped by the villainess, then a capture target saves the heroine. Ah! That's what I need to do! I need to tell a capture target that I can't find Maria and send him forward on his quest! I am so smart! Maria is lucky she has me to be her best friend! So who do I go to? Sadly Simon is out of the question. I just sent him to the library. The professor is still on the hell no list. That leaves Duke Victor, Prince Levi, and Sir Grey. I don't particularly like Duke Victor, so sorry buddy, you're getting a veto. Actually, Prince Levi is the best choice. By telling him it will automatically inform Sir Grey. There's a better chance one of the two of them will find her! I puff up with pride. Haha! Take that game! I know your secrets! Now, let's go save the heroine!

www.ingramcontent.com/pod-product-compliance
Lightning Source LLC
Chambersburg PA
CBHW072208070526
44585CB00015B/1241